The Centralisation of Western Europe

*The Common Market,
Political Integration, and Democracy*

ROLAND VAUBEL

*Professor of Economics,
University of Mannheim*

Published by
INSTITUTE OF ECONOMIC AFFAIRS
1995

First published in February 1995

by

THE INSTITUTE OF ECONOMIC AFFAIRS
2 Lord North Street, Westminster,
London SW1P 3LB

© THE INSTITUTE OF ECONOMIC AFFAIRS 1995

Hobart Paper 127

All rights reserved

ISSN 0073-2818

ISBN 0-255 36343-5 ✓

Cover design by David Lucas

Printed in Great Britain by
BOURNE PRESS LIMITED, BOURNEMOUTH, DORSET
Set in Baskerville Roman 11 on 12 point

CONTENTS

[3]

FOREWORD

Debate about the future direction of the European Union is intensifying, not only in Britain but also in other European countries, as the 1996 Inter-Governmental Conference approaches. The original idea of the Community – as an organisation which brought down trade barriers and created an internal market in Europe – has come to be widely accepted. But there is much less of a consensus that the present 'Union' should travel farther in its recent direction of developing central economic and social policies and seeking competence in defence and foreign affairs.

The media often portrays this debate as one in which Britain stands reluctantly aside from its partners, all of whom wish to move rapidly towards greater integration. But that is inaccurate. In each country there is a variety of views, even though some of Europe's most prominent politicians make it appear that nothing but unbounded enthusiasm for further centralisation exists in their countries.

To obtain a view from outside Britain the Institute commissioned the eminent German economist, Professor Roland Vaubel, to examine whether or not there is a case for the assumption by the Union of greater and greater powers. Could such powers be justified, for example, on grounds of economies of scale or scope or because there is a need for harmonisation to ensure 'fair' competition?

In *Hobart Paper* No.127, Professor Vaubel begins (Section I) by explaining why classical liberals prefer decentralised decision-making to centralisation: individual preferences can be satisfied and competition among governments protects individual freedom. Market integration is desirable but 'political integration' stifles competition and suppresses preferences.

He writes:

> '...the liberalisation of markets is used as a pretext for the centralisation of policies even though it will restrict competition and threaten individual liberty.' (p.13)

Vaubel turns in Section II to a rigorous analysis, using a large body of theory and empirical evidence, of the arguments used to justify centralising decisions. It is, for example, claimed there should be 'harmonisation' of social regulations, taxes,

[7]

environmental standards and support for industry and agriculture in the interests of reducing market distortions. But, Professor Vaubel argues,

> 'Uniform European regulations do not remove international distortions of competition; they create such distortions.' (p.19)

There may be a case for an independent European competition agency (detached from the Commission) and for international (not necessarily EU) action to combat cross-border externalities. But, in Vaubel's view,

> '...the European Union has obtained a number of competencies which, under an efficient division of labour, belong to the member-states, lower levels of government or individual citizens.' (p.33)

Why then does centralisation occur if it cannot be justified on economic efficiency grounds? Professor Vaubel turns to the theory of public choice, of which he is a distinguished exponent, for an explanation. In his view, centralisation results from a flawed political structure within which bureaucrats, politicians and judges pursue their own interests. Thus, central government grows within the Union for the same reason as it has been found to grow within a single country.

But in a Union with such a primitive political structure the tendency for government expansion is even greater than in individual member-states. The European Commission is a bureaucracy which is not confined to administration but is part of the legislative process within which it has the monopoly of initiative; the European Parliament 'reinforces the Commission's centralising tendencies' (p.37); the European Court of Justice is an 'engine' of integration; the Council of Ministers, as a 'European cartel of politicians' (p.41), seeks bargaining power *vis-à-vis* non-members and can evade Parliamentary control.

Moreover, the influence of special interest groups is increased because they can lobby one instead of 15 governments and because centralisation increases the costs of obtaining information to the individuals who have to foot the bill. Given the present political structure, there is a ratchet effect which means that centralising measures are difficult to reverse. Indeed, the ratchet is recognised in the doctrine of *acquis communautaire*.

What is to be done? Professor Vaubel is sceptical whether the Union can be re-invented from scratch. The most promising approach, in his view, is to build on the subsidiarity principle in the Maastricht Treaty but 'The crucial question is who is going to interpret it' (p.58). The interpreters should not be (as at present) the Commission, the Council and the European Court of Justice, all of which '...have a vested interest in centralisation' (p.58). Instead, national parliaments should control Union legislation: all directives and regulations not within the Union's exclusive competence should be approved by the parliaments of member-states.

Professor Vaubel also sees a place for referenda on issues such as the size of the Union budget, partial opt-outs and secession. He would like to see a unanimity rule in the Council when powers are transferred from member-states to the Union. The European Court should be reformed, perhaps adding a Court of Review charged with interpreting subsidiarity cases. The Commission should no longer be the 'legislative agenda setter' (p.69), all quasi-judicial functions should be removed from it and it should be supervised by the Council of Ministers.

In Section V, Professor Vaubel points to the increasing realisation that 'what seemed to start as a purely economic undertaking is really meant to attain political objectives' (p.71). The Union can no longer draw its legitimation from individual freedom as it could when it was pursuing market integration. The legitimacy of policy centralisation can be derived only from democracy – which is what the Union lacks. Present European institutions

> '...have a vested interest in continuing on the path of creeping centralisation'. (p.72)

The democratic deficit is no coincidence – '...powerful actors benefit from it'. Therefore the '...only effective cure is institutional and procedural reform' (p.73), stemming from the initiative of the parliaments of member-states.

The Institute of Economic Affairs has no corporate view: the views expressed in this *Hobart Paper* are those of the author, not of the Institute, its Trustees, Directors or Advisers. Professor Vaubel's compelling and provocative *tour de force* is published as an important contribution to discussions about the future of Europe.

February 1995   COLIN ROBINSON
Editorial Director, Institute of Economic Affairs;
Professor of Economics, University of Surrey

THE AUTHOR

ROLAND VAUBEL is Professor of Economics at the University of Mannheim, Germany. He received a BA in Philosophy, Politics and Economics from the University of Oxford, an MA in economics from Columbia University, New York, and a doctorate in economics from the University of Kiel, Germany. He has been a researcher at the Institute of World Economics, University of Kiel (West Germany), Professor of Monetary Economics at Erasmus University, Rotterdam, and Visiting Professor in International Economics at the University of Chicago (Graduate School of Business). He is a member of the Academic Advisory Council of the German Ministry of Economics, an adjunct scholar of Cato Institute, Washington D.C., and a member of the Academic Advisory Council of the Institute of Economic Affairs.

Professor Vaubel specialises in international finance, international organisations, public choice and social policy. His publications include *Strategies for Currency Unification. The Economics of Currency Competition and the Case for a European Parallel Currency* (1978); and *The Political Economy of International Organizations* (1991), which he co-edited with Th.D. Willett. The IEA published his Wincott Memorial Lecture, *Choice in European Monetary Union* (IEA Occasional Paper No.55, 1979).

I. INTRODUCTION

'Ten years hence, 80 per cent of our economic legislation, and perhaps even our fiscal and social legislation as well, will be of Community origin.'

(Jacques Delors, Debates of the European Parliament, 6 July 1988, No. 2-367/140.)

From a classical liberal perspective, decentralised decision-making is preferable to centralisation for two principal reasons.

The *first* is that individual preferences differ. The classical liberal respects individual preferences and wants them to be satisfied as much as possible. They are his ultimate measuring-rod. The most decentralised system of decision-making is the market. But differences of preferences are just as important in the field of public policy. The demand for 'public' goods and services and the supply of voluntary transfers depend on income levels, geographic conditions and social traditions which have shaped local and regional preferences.

Income is the factor that can be measured most easily. In the European Union, income per head is about three times as high in the most prosperous member-countries (Luxembourg and Denmark) as it is in the poorest member-countries (Portugal and Greece). Between the richest and the poorest region of the European Union the ratio is as much as six to one. Regional disparities are also far larger in the European Union than in the United States of America. The Gini coefficient[1] of *per capita* GDP is 0·072 for the 48 contiguous US states but 0·130 for the 59 regions of the European Union.[2]

International differences in policy preferences are revealed by comparative opinion polls. This *Hobart Paper* considers some

---

[1] The Gini coefficient measures the deviation from income equality. A value of 0 indicates complete equality, a value of 1 complete inequality.

[2] Although students of economics learn what the income elasticity of demand is, the implications for the decentralisation of government are rarely spelt out.

of these results to see how they are correlated with income levels and other variables that determine preferences.

Decentralisation: the Power of 'Exit' and 'Voice'

The *second* reason for decentralisation is that competition among governments protects the freedom of the individual. Competing governments are constrained by the 'exit' and 'voice'[3] of their citizens.

If economic policy is decentralised, some people vote with their feet and many vote with their money and capital. This is *exit*. Max Weber, Eric Jones and others[4] have shown that competition among governments for financial, physical and human capital is the key to understanding why the enlightenment, the rise of science and the Industrial Revolution took place in Europe and not in China or India which, in the Middle Ages, had been at a similar level of civilisation. The European Union, by contrast, aims at common minimum tax rates and regulations rather than diversity and competition.

Voice is any form of protest that operates through the political process. Like exit, it is a corrective feedback mechanism. It is strengthened by decentralisation because diversity increases the scope for comparison and choice and because the citizen's incentive to be informed is stronger in a smaller polity.

Whereas the exit option protects minorities, voice ensures democratic control. Both are ways of finding out what citizens want. They facilitate the control of bureaucracy and weaken the influence of organised interest groups. Several econometric studies[5] confirm that government expenditure is smaller relative

---

[3] The terms 'exit' and 'voice' are due to Albert O. Hirschman: see, for example, his article 'Exit, Voice and the State', in A.O. Hirschman, *Essays in Trespassing Economics to Politics and Beyond*, Cambridge: Cambridge University Press, 1981, pp.266-84.

[4] Max Weber, *General Economic History*, New York: Collier, 1961, p.249; Eric L. Jones, *The European Miracle*, Cambridge: Cambridge University Press, 1981, Ch.6; John A. Hall, *Powers and Liberties: The Causes and the Consequences of the Rise of the West*, Oxford: Blackwell, 1985, esp. p.102; Daniel Chirot, *Social Change in the Modern Era*, San Diego, etc.: Harcourt Brace Jovanovich, 1986, esp. p.296; Nathan Rosenberg, L.E. Birdzell, *How the West Grew Rich*, New York: Basic Books, 1986, esp. pp.136 ff.; Paul Kennedy, *The Rise and Fall of the Great Powers*, New York: Random House, 1987, esp. pp.19 f.

[5] For time-series analyses see M.L. Marlow, 'Fiscal Decentralization and Government Size', *Public Choice*, Vol.56, 1988, pp.259-69; and P.J. Grossman,

to GDP, the more government expenditure itse   ⌐
decentralised.

In the European context, centralisation is cal
integration. It has to be distinguished from market
While competition is increased by market integratio𝗇, ɪ𝗍 ɪ𝗌 ᴜ𝗇𝗅𝖾
by political integration. Market integration respects, and is
guided by, differences in preferences but political integration
ignores and suppresses them. That is why political integration,
unlike market integration, can easily go too far. Integration is a
weasel word that is easily abused: the positive connotation of
market integration is automatically transferred to political
integration, and the liberalisation of markets is used as a pretext
for the centralisation of policies even though it will restrict
competition and threaten individual liberty.

The distinction between market integration and political
integration is often confused with the distinction between
widening and deepening but the two are quite different.
Deepening can also refer to market integration (as in the case
of the Internal Market Programme), and widening can be
confined to political integration. For the classical liberal, the
crucial distinction is between market and political integration.

The two reasons for decentralisation interact: to the extent
that people vote with their feet, preferences within regions
become more homogeneous.

The classical liberal is not concerned only with the demand
side (the freedom and preferences of the individual). As Hayek
has shown, decentralisation and competition also favour
progress on the supply side. The diversity of contemporaneous
experiments in the market and in public policy facilitates
learning by discovery and imitation. Moreover, diversification in
supply is a way of reducing risk.

Classical Liberal and Nationalist: Fundamental Disagreements

In the European context, the classical liberal's warnings against
undue centralisation are often confused with nationalism. Quite
apart from the different philosophical origins, however, the

'Fiscal Decentralization and Government Size: An Extension', *Public Choice*,
Vol.62, 1989, pp.63-69. The cross-section studies have been surveyed by D.
Joulfaian, M.L. Marlow, *Applied Economics*, Vol.23, 1991, pp.1,603-12. An
international cross-section analysis can also be found in my article 'The Political
Economy of Centralisation and the European Community', *Public Choice*, Vol.81,
1994, pp.151-90, Table 2.

classical liberal and the nationalist are in fundamental disagreement in at least four respects.

- The nationalist is an admirer of the state, in his case the nation state. The classical liberal distrusts the state.

- The nationalist is not necessarily in favour of decentralisation. He opposes centralisation at the supra-national level but welcomes it at the level of the nation state. The classical liberal, by contrast, is consistent in his plea for decentralisation. He also wants to transfer powers from the national to the provincial and from the provincial to the local level. He is an advocate of devolution within the member-states.

- The nationalist is proud of his own country and considers it better than others. The classical liberal may not be proud of anything. He may be indifferent among countries or prefer a foreign country. But he insists that individuals and groups of individuals differ, and he wishes them to be free to pursue their own goals.

- The nationalist wants his own nation to prevail over other nations, including distributional gains at the expense of other nations. The classical liberal, by contrast, aims at 'Pareto improvements' which make some better off whilst nobody is worse off. For him, peaceful competition is a positive sum game in which everybody will gain in the longer run. Most advocates of European political centralisation want to strengthen Europe's influence in world affairs and its bargaining position *vis-à-vis* the United States, Japan and others. Europe is to become a world power. They are not liberals but Euro-chauvinists. They have not overcome nationalism but are merely transferring it to a higher (European) level. The classical liberal, by contrast, is a cosmopolitan.

This *Hobart Paper* analyses European centralisation from a classical liberal perspective. Section II defines normative criteria for an appropriate division of labour between international organisations and the member-states and applies them to the European Union. It shows that these criteria are violated in a considerable number of policy fields. (Non-economists may wish to skip the more technical parts of this section.) Section III uses the theory of public choice to explain such government failures and the underlying dynamics of centralisation. Section IV derives proposals for constitutional reform that could bring about an efficient equilibrium consistent with subsidiarity. Section V argues that the Inter-Governmental Conference of 1996 may prove a window of opportunity for such a reform.

II. EFFICIENCY CRITERIA

Centralisation is the enemy of individual freedom but it can be efficient if certain conditions are met. None of these conditions is sufficient for centralisation to be desirable but if it were desirable at least one of them must hold. Economists agree on three such conditions. Centralisation may be efficient:

(i)   if decentralised policy-making restricts or distorts competition;

(ii)   if it generates interjurisdictional non-market externalities; or

(iii)   if it fails to exploit economies of scale or scope.

But as the example of the European Union shows, these criteria are frequently misinterpreted and misapplied.

Free and Undistorted Competition

If competition is restricted by barriers to trade and movements of factors (such as labour and capital), or if it is distorted by national regulations, taxes and subsidies, international co-operation can improve the allocation of resources – especially if it is not confined to 15 countries (as it is in the EU) but takes place at the global level. The European Union has made considerable progress in removing internal barriers but it has erected new and particularly vicious non-tariff barriers against the rest of the world. While this is well known, extreme confusion surrounds the concept of 'competitive distortion', a term used to justify any attempt to reduce the differences in regulations, taxes and subsidies among the member-states. However, as a few examples will show, many of these differences are not distortions at all but reflect differences in preferences and factor endowments.

Social Regulations and Transfers

The European Commission and the signatories of the Social Chapter aim at common minimum requirements with respect, for example, to the health and safety of workers, working conditions in general, the social protection of workers, the termination of employment contracts, the collective defence of workers' interests, social insurance, and so on. These minimum requirements tend to exceed the lowest existing national standard. They reduce the differences among the national regulations and increase the average intensity of regulation in the Union. Both effects are undesirable.

Social regulation of the labour, housing, insurance market, health care and similar markets tends to be based on three arguments: imperfect competition, asymmetric information and 'time inconsistency'.

Imperfect Competition

If there is only one supplier or buyer or a cartel of suppliers or buyers, regulation is supposed to eliminate the resulting inefficiency and distributional effect by prescribing the price that would prevail under perfect competition. The problem with this argument is that, in the absence of competition, the government does not and cannot know the price that would prevail under competition. Moreover, if pricing is politicised, interest groups or the 'median voter'[1] may induce the government to err on the opposite side and to make things worse than they would have been without regulation. If the government sets too low a price, quality deteriorates (for example, in housing) and has to be regulated as well. A consumer whose choice is restricted by a monopoly is not likely to benefit if the government, by regulation, restricts his choice even further. If competition is seriously deficient, the appropriate instrument is competition policy, not regulation. It is the only way of finding the competitive price, and it can be assigned to a non-political quasi-judicial institution.

Asymmetric Information

Similarly, if asymmetric information is the problem, the government cannot do better unless it can acquire the missing information at lower cost. However, if this condition were satisfied, it would be sufficient for the government to disclose

---

[1] The median voter takes the middle position so that there is an equal number of voters on both sides. Thus, under majority rule, the winning party or coalition has to gain the support of the median voter. For the redistributive implications of the median voter theorem see, notably, George J. Stigler, 'Director's Law of Public Income Redistribution', *Journal of Law and Economics*, Vol.13, 1970, pp.1-10; and Gordon Tullock, *The Vote Motive*, Hobart Paperback No.9, London: Institute of Economic Affairs, 1976.

this information. Regulation is neither necessary nor desirable.

Time Inconsistency

The 'time inconsistency' argument is used to justify compulsory periods of notice and co-determination laws. Otherwise, the argument runs, workers would not be willing to acquire sufficient job-specific skills. However, since both workers and employers are interested in job-specific training, they would in any event agree on periods of notice and an efficient arbitration procedure for dismissals. The rôle of the government is to enforce, not to regulate, these contracts.

Regulation is justified only where negative externalities cannot be internalised by liability rules because the damage is irreversible or because the liable person cannot be identified or is unable to pay compensation. Elementary health and safety standards, an obligation to be vaccinated against dangerous contagious diseases, or an obligation to insure against catastrophic risks may be of this type.

Thus, if the international integration of markets undermines the regulatory power of national governments, far from constituting a problem it is usually an important benefit of market integration which restores freedom of contract. To the extent that regulations are consistent with local preferences, the differences can survive the increased mobility of capital and labour.

Even those who believe that social regulations do more good than harm and that they are not inferior to other policy instruments must recognise the inefficiency of reducing international differences among social regulations. The problem is not just that, by raising regulations, say, in Portugal, the policy-makers of the Union generate additional unemployment in Portugal. Even if wages in Portugal dropped so as to offset the additional regulatory cost to employers, Portuguese workers would be worse off because the preferred number of working hours, length of vacation, degree of security and working environment depend on income, geographical conditions, social traditions, and other local factors. The correlation with income is clearly apparent from opinion polls among the member-states. The non-pecuniary component of the return from working would be too large, while the wage component and the supply of labour would be too small. Since social regulation is supposed to enforce the conditions that would prevail under perfect competition and symmetric information, and since demand and supply conditions differ among the member-countries, national optima will clearly differ. *Uniform European regulations do not remove international distortions of competition; they create such distortions.*

Nor do they prevent 'social dumping'. Dumping is price discrimination or selling below cost. But Portuguese workers do not engage in price discrimination nor do they sell below cost. Their opportunity cost *is* lower. That is their comparative advantage. To suppress it is to misallocate resources and prevent those workers from catching up with the others.

Even those who believe in more widespread social regulation at the national level, must surely admit that the imperfections of competition – one of their reasons for regulation – are reduced by the increased mobility of capital and labour which market integration brings about. Moreover, their distrust of competitive deregulation under market integration does not justify more uniform social regulation. For their purposes, it would be sufficient to conclude an international agreement that no member-state may lower its social regulations without the assent of its partners.

Differences in preferences and factor endowments also militate against a levelling of welfare payments, mandatory social insurance benefits, vocational training and consumer protection.

Social benefits must be related to local market wages because of the 'moral hazard' problem. Moreover, redistributive preferences differ. If, in spite of language barriers, welfare recipients turned out to be mobile in a common labour market, they could remain the financial responsibility of their home country even after they had left it (on the origin principle). Ideally, the host country would disburse the welfare payments and social insurance benefits obtainable in the country of origin and be reimbursed by it. International differences of benefits could then be maintained without inducing inefficient migration, international migration externalities or a competitive lowering of benefits. History shows that this type of arrangement is clearly workable. But it is unlikely to be necessary. Even within federal states like Switzerland and Canada where social policy is highly

[19]

centralised, 'welfare tourism' is not a problem, and redistribution is considerable.

The optimal level of insurance and consumer protection also depends on risk aversion and indirectly on income. For example, there is no need to 'harmonise' the guarantees for bank deposits and investment funds in the member-states. Similarly, the optimal scheme for vocational training depends on the country's factor endowments and comparative advantage. Such differences are not distorting and should not be levelled.

Environmental Protection

International differences among environmental standards are also regarded as distortions of competition. The European Union is supposed to reduce these differences by imposing minimum standards even where pollution is not of the border-crossing type. However, environmental preferences differ. They have been shown to depend, for example, on income, population density and age.[2] Among the member-states of the European Union, population density varies even more than income (between 361 inhabitants per sq. km. in the Netherlands and 15 in Finland). The optimal level of pollution depends also on the availability of unpolluted resources and natural cleansing capacities (historical and geographic factors). For all these reasons, uniform environmental standards or taxes are likely to be inefficient. Not the diversity of environmental policies but their suppression constitutes a distortion. As we shall see, this also has implications for the problem of border-crossing pollution.

Agricultural Policy

Subsidies to agriculture may be justified, if at all, on social or environmental grounds.[3] As we have seen, however, welfare

---

[2] A cross-section analysis for the member-states of the European Union yields clearly positive correlations between the share of those who favour a decisive strengthening of environmental protection (*Eurobarometer*, 1979, 1981) and national GDP *per capita* or population density. (The simple correlation coefficients are 0·35 and 0·31, respectively, for the logarithms. I report the simple correlation coefficients because the two explanatory variables are highly colinear.)

[3] Security of supply is not a convincing justification because individual consumers can secure their supply by holding inventories or by concluding forward and insurance contracts and because they differ in their risk aversion.

[20]

payments ought to be related to the local wage rate the recipients could earn in alternative employment, and the appropriate compensation for environmental services depends on the local demand for these services. Since both wage rates and environmental preferences differ considerably among the member-states, it is inefficient to centralise agricultural policy at the Union level. The transfer payments to farmers should not only be independent of production but also differentiated by region.

The Subsidisation and Regulation of Industry

The same is true for subsidies to industry which compensate for positive externalities, optimise the supply of natural monopoly goods[4] or guarantee a minimum income for workers. However, subsidies to industry are rarely of this sort. They are usually provided in response to rent-seeking by domestic special-interest groups. They distort competition. The same is true for national public procurement policies and regulations which discriminate in favour of domestic suppliers. Since national governments tend to be exempt from national competition policies, the control of such subsidies, regulations and government purchases is a proper task for an international organisation (the European Union or, even better, the OECD or GATT). The liberal conception of Europe is not confined to the removal of barriers to trade and factor movements. It also requires an authority that enforces the rules of competition among governments. But, unlike the European Commission, such an international competition authority ought to be a non-political quasi-judicial body, which should not be permitted to introduce subsidies or regulations itself. Otherwise, its decisions will be biased. It will use its power to create room for Union subsidies and regulations which are likely to do even more damage. Union institutions, for instance, in the field of subsidy control, are not subject to the rules which they impose on the member-states. Moreover, Union rules discriminate in favour of the member-states: for

---

[4] If marginal cost is below average cost and if the product is traded internationally, the opening of markets reduces the incentive to provide the optimal subsidy unless exported national subsidies are reimbursed by the recipient country.

example, in the case of government procurement, they provide for a 3 per cent preference in favour of EC suppliers and a 50 per cent EC content requirement.

Taxation

Are international differences in tax rates necessarily distortions of competition as the European Commission evidently believes (with the support of many economists)? The European Union has introduced a minimum rate of value-added tax. Common minimum rates have also been proposed for corporate income tax (by the Ruding Committee in 1992), for the motor vehicle tax (by the European Commission in 1992), and for the withholding tax on interest and dividends (by some member-states). However, according to the theory of optimum taxation, the welfare loss from taxation and the optimal tax rate depend on the price elasticities of demand and supply. Since the price elasticities of demand and of labour supply depend on income, the wide income discrepancies that exist among the member-states point against uniform tax rates. Furthermore, factor mobility *vis-à-vis* other jurisdictions depends on the factor combination and the relative size of the home country. Finally, the cost and effectiveness of tax collection is known to vary among the member-states. Quite apart from the beneficial effects of tax competition, differences in preferences, factor endowments and technologies call for a differentiation of tax structures and rates of taxation.

Monetary and Exchange Rate Policy

The elimination of price distortions has also been advanced as an argument in favour of monetary union. As long as the member-states have separate currencies, national monetary policies may be abused for beggar-thy-neighbour purposes: unexpected depreciation can serve to gain a temporary competitive advantage, while an unexpected appreciation is a way of temporarily importing price stability. Even if these effects are not intended, but merely the by-product of an unexpected monetary policy aimed at domestic targets, they temporarily distort international relative prices.

Quite apart from the benefits of currency competition, which promotes price level stability, the above argument is, however, deficient in two respects.

[22]

First, it ignores the fact that member-states face differential shocks and, owing to their structural and income differences, are differently affected by identical shocks. Such asymmetric changes of demand and supply require adjustments of international relative prices which are achieved at lowest cost by nominal exchange rate adjustment. German unification was an asymmetric shock of this sort. The economic transformation of Eastern Europe will affect the European Union in a similar way but on a much larger scale: since Eastern Europe will primarily export agricultural and labour-intensive products, the currencies of the agrarian and labour-abundant member-states of the European Union will have to depreciate against the others in real terms. There will also be a differential impact with respect to natural resources. Not all exchange rate changes distort relative prices; on the contrary, they can be equilibrating.

Second, there are other remedies against beggar-thy-neighbour policies short of blocking exchange rate adjustment. National central banks could be given full independence and strong incentives to avoid unexpected monetary policies. Ideally, the members of the central bank council would receive terms of office that extend to their retirement age, and they would be dismissed if, over several years, the average inflation rate exceeded a certain limit or if the price level dropped. After all, such precautions would also be required for a European Central Bank if beggar-thy-neighbour policies against non-members were to be avoided.

International Externalities

Interjurisdictional spillovers can justify international co-operation at the European level but the argument tends to be misapplied in three respects:

- not all international spillovers impair efficiency;

- not all which do ought to be tackled at the European level; and

- even those which require European co-operation may not justify centralisation or convergence of policies.

Is Efficiency Impaired?

International spillovers which merely operate through the price mechanism in competitive markets are not sufficient to establish a case for international policy co-operation, let alone centralisation. On the contrary, international price arbitrage in interdependent markets is precisely the mechanism by which efficiency is attained. The fact that, say, packaging waste or liability insurance is traded among the member-states of the European Union does not justify Union directives in these fields. By contrast, international co-operation is clearly required in the case of sizeable international non-market spillovers, for example, if air or water *pollution* crosses international borders. By implication, it is not required to deal with domestic pollution problems such as noise and the quality of drinking water. Nevertheless, the Community has adopted a directive with regard to drinking water (1980).

In recent years, some game theorists[5] have tried to extend the case for international policy co-operation to cases of mere market interdependence. They have notably called for international bargaining over *monetary and fiscal policy*. Their analyses rest on the crucial assumption that policy-makers pursue, and are justified in pursuing, more targets than they have instruments.[6] From a classical liberal perspective, this assumption is unacceptable. Effective control of policy-makers requires a clear assignment of responsibilities. If, for this reason, one target is chosen for each instrument and if each instrument is assigned to the target for which it has a 'comparative advantage', decentralised decision-making is fully efficient. In the case of mere market interdependence, the assignment solution is preferable to international policy collusion.

Competition Policy

A more complicated case is *competition policy*. The international spillover, it is true, is transmitted through market prices but

---

[5] For a simple exposition of the argument see Gilles Oudiz, 'Macroeconomic Policy Coordination: Where Should We Stand?', in Herbert Giersch (ed.), *Macro and Micro Policies for More Growth and Employment*, Tuebingen: Mohr/Siebeck, 1988, pp.278-91.

[6] The assumption is a necessary but not a sufficient condition for international policy co-operation to be optimal. Even if the assumption is satisfied, international co-operation among policy-makers can be counterproductive, for example, because it fuels inflation expectations. This is the so-called Rogoff paradox. (Kenneth Rogoff, 'Can International Monetary Policy Cooperation Be Counterproductive?', *Journal of International Economics*, Vol. 18, 1985, pp. 199-217.)

the markets in question are by definition not competitive. Thus, where competition is restricted and distorted by cartels, monopolies and other dominant firms, the competition policy of one country may generate efficiency gains in all countries. If competition policy is simply left to national authorities, they may supply too little of it and behave as free-riders. Thus, some form of international co-operation is required in competition policy.

However, the national competition authorities are better informed about competitive conditions in their own country. In Germany, there are even provincial anti-cartel authorities. Thus, there is a trade-off between the internalisation of external effects and the efficient use of information. In theory, both can be reconciled if all like-minded countries conclude an international agreement which obliges them to enforce competition according to common rules but leaves the application and implementation to them. If each national authority provides for workable competition in its own country, competition is also workable in the common market. In practice, however, two complications arise. Both concern the enforcement of the common rules.

First, clarification is required of who is responsible for cartels and mergers among firms from different member-states. In principle, responsibility could simply be assigned to the member-state in which the largest participating firm is incorporated. The decisions of its competition authority could be enforced by the other member-states on the principle of mutual recognition.[7] Only if the other countries feared that their interests would not sufficiently be taken into account would these cases have to be handled by a common international competition authority. The anti-cartel policy of the European Union, however, is not confined to cartels among firms from different member-states. Its merger control is subject to the condition that the participating firms must not achieve more than two-thirds of their individual union-wide turnover within a common member-state. Their location is irrelevant.

The *second* enforcement problem is that some national competition authorities may violate the commonly agreed

---

[7] Australia and New Zealand, for example, recognise each other's competition policies under their Closer Economic Relations Agreement.

s. Since they might continue to be too lenient in domestic
s, there is a valid case for a supra-national competition
authority that can act as a court of appeal and require tougher
sanctions. As German competition policy shows, a two-step
procedure can be very efficient. The European Union follows
a one-step procedure. The Commission is not a court of
appeal but it directly handles competition cases. It is a
political, not a judicial, body. The final decision is taken not by
economic experts but in a secret majority vote of the 20
Commissioners. Lack of transparency in the decision-making
process favours large, well-informed firms and encourages
rent-seeking. Nor is the Commission's rôle confined to
imposing stricter competition standards; when it has decided a
case, the national competition authority is not permitted to be
tougher. The law of the Union is supreme. European
competition policy is considered less strict than, for example,
German competition policy. For this reason, it is preferred by
German industry. Many economists fear that it will be used to
make room for the European industrial policy introduced by
the Treaty of Maastricht. *The European Commission has become the
sole supplier of Union-wide monopoly rights.*

If competition policy is handed over to an independent
European competition agency, that institution could also
obtain jurisdiction over interested associated countries such as
the states of Eastern Europe. Since the European Union tries
to justify its anti-dumping policy on the ground that foreign
countries do not have an adequate competition policy,
associated countries which accepted the jurisdiction of the
Union competition authority would have to be exempted from
these foreign trade restrictions of the Union.

The Appropriate Level of Co-operation

Because there are genuine externalities among member-
countries, it does not follow that the European Union is the
appropriate level for international arrangements to internalise
them. *Defence* is a good example. The defence policy of one
country, say, Britain, generates positive external effects for
many other countries, not just the other members of the
European Union. Thus, defence is efficiently provided in a
wider international framework that incorporates all like-
minded beneficiaries, such as NATO. A competing European
defence or security policy is even likely to undermine NATO.

It may be that NATO is not well-equipped to deal with the new situation in Eastern Europe. From the point of view of externality theory, however, the efficient response is not to introduce a rival defence policy at a lower level but to extend the existing security system to the East. Defence arrangements have to become more encompassing, not less. Analogous considerations apply to foreign policy.

If it turned out that, for political reasons, Eastern European states cannot become members of NATO but only of the European Union, rivalries between NATO and the European Union could be avoided by confining the latter to issues which the other members of NATO do not want to take up. But this would be an invitation to American free-riding and isolationism.

In the course of history, most political and defence alliances have been established under a common external threat. Since the threat from the East has been diminishing, the common European foreign and security policy should probably not be regarded as a step towards closer international integration but as the beginning of the disintegration of the North Atlantic Alliance.

There are many other examples of such wider externalities, for example, the fight against *international crime, contagious diseases*[8] and *ocean and air pollution*, property rights for *ocean fishing, competition policy*, the promotion of *basic research*,[9] and *development aid*. In all these fields, the externalities are world-wide, and European solutions are likely to be inadequate. Wherever feasible, world organisations (like Interpol, the World Health Organisation, the United Nations, GATT, the World Bank), or at least common institutions of all like-minded industrial countries (OECD) would, in principle, be preferable.

To avoid an undue concentration of political power and a centralising dynamic, it is important to have a considerable

---

[8] There is no case for a general European competence in the field of health. The European directives on working time and tobacco advertising, for example, are not justified by significant international health externalities.

[9] The research and development policy of the European Union discriminates in favour of European projects but it is also inefficient for another reason: it tries to pick the winners, which it cannot do. The efficient instrument would be a uniform subsidy to all basic research.

[27]

number of different international organisations which specialise in their sphere of competence and comprise different memberships reflecting the range of the externality in question.

International externalities may not only transcend the borders of the European Union; they may alternatively be limited to only a few member-countries. *Pollution of rivers* (the Rhine) *or lakes* (Lake Constance) is a good example. International *roads, railway lines* and *pipelines* are also mostly bilateral problems. Significant international spillovers from *regional policy* – most of which are merely due to market interdependence anyway – tend to be confined to one or two countries. In all these instances, bilateral or small group solutions are more efficient than Union policies. Only if a clear majority of the member-countries is significantly affected may the Union be a more appropriate level of decision-making.

What is true for the negotiation of treaties need not hold for their *enforcement*, however. Even agreements among sub-groups of member-states can usefully be enforced by institutions of the Union. The Treaty of Maastricht contains a number of examples. The Union is likely to have a comparative advantage in providing mutual trust and an international legal order: liberalising trade and factor movements is a case in point.

Co-operating When Preferences Differ

Centralisation and equalisation of policies tend to be inefficient when preferences differ on a geographical basis. This is also true in the presence of international externalities. The only exception is the case of pure international public goods, that is, policies which are bound to affect all member-states identically. They constitute an interesting theoretical construct, the extreme case of a positive externality. In the real world, however, they are hard to come by. The supply of public goods can differ among countries and regions.

Environmental protection may serve as an example (even though, strictly speaking, it does not generate a positive externality but removes a negative one – pollution). Since the demand for a clean environment rises with income, population density and other factors, and since these determinants differ very considerably among the member-states, the price to polluters of contaminating air and water ought to vary accordingly. However, the individual member-state should not be permitted to discriminate between pollution of domestic and foreign origin. Both must be priced in the same way, either by levying pollution charges or, if possible, by selling pollution vouchers.[10] Since the marginal disutility of pollution[11] tends to increase with quantity, the price to polluters has to rise with the intensity of the emission. International price differentials, it is true, will induce international relocations. But even if international arbitrage was perfect so as to equalise the price of pollution *ex post* at the margin, the quantity of emissions would differ among countries according to their preferences.

As usual in the case of externalities, the efficient solution implies compensation payments, not regulation – let alone uniform standards. The rôle of the international organisation is to measure the international externalities, to outlaw price discrimination against foreigners, to enforce international compensation, and possibly to settle the accounts in a multilateral clearing system. The Council has agreed that, from 1997 onwards, the international compensation payments of VAT revenue will be handled by a clearing system of the Union. International pollution can be dealt with in a similar way. Common environmental (minimum) standards are neither necessary nor efficient.

These considerations can also be applied to positive international externalities, for example, to *development aid* and other forms of *foreign policy* or of *charitable transfers*. If bilateral development aid and domestic social transfers increase the utility of other potential donors, but to a lesser degree, and if free-riding on other people's generosity reduces gifts to below the donors' own optimum, the externalities could be internalised by a system of mutual intergovernmental matching grants. As in the case of environmental policy and VAT, the international organisations could operate a multilateral clearing system. At first glance, this solution might

---

[10] There is, of course, no guarantee that these prices will be an honest and accurate reflection of preferences. However, the same problem arises if the countries bargain or vote for common European standards.

[11] The marginal disutility of pollution is the damage or loss of utility due to one additional unit of pollution, for instance, a cubic foot of sulphur dioxide.

seem cumbersome. But it merely renders explicit the aggregation of preferences which any efficient policy presupposes. Even if economies of scale justified a common policy, say, of foreign aid, a procedure would have to be found to allow for different donor preferences. The technical revolution in communications and data processing has strengthened the case for co-ordination rather than centralisation.

International Economies of Scale and Scope

Centralisation at the European level may be efficient if it reduces the cost of existing public policies. The economies may be related to the quantity of supply (economies of scale), the number of users (social economies of scale as with club goods), or the number of jointly-produced policies (economies of scope). The argument does not presuppose that these policies exert international external effects.

International economies of scale are frequently confused with more international bargaining power. If there are, say, three countries and two of them combine, they can improve their bargaining position *vis-à-vis* the third, but these are not economies of scale. Economies of scale presuppose an increase in efficiency (a Pareto-improvement). Collusion among the two countries does not generate efficiency gains but distributional gains at the expense of the third country. By combining, European countries can, for example, increase their political 'clout' *vis-à-vis* the United States or Japan. But there is no reason to believe that the outcome is better for the world as a whole. If the policies of the third country tend to be more reasonable than the policies of the European partners, the outcome for the world is indeed likely to be worse. The common security, foreign and commercial policies of the European Union may be cases in point. It is even doubtful whether such common policies reduce the transaction costs of negotiation because, before negotiating with the third country, the European countries still have to negotiate with each other.

Nevertheless, there may be international economies of scale in some of these fields. *Defence* is a likely candidate because joint design and procurement of weapons can reduce the cost of production and deployment. In *foreign policy*, joint embassies may save on fixed costs, and the same may be true for *development aid*. Like international externalities, however, such international economies of scale are not likely to be limited to the European Union.

If preferences differ in the presence of scale economies, joint decision-making tends to require unanimity, or those who disagree must be free to opt out. The decision cannot be left to the median voter because he is not representative. If preferences differ only with respect to quantity, the international organisation could be the sole supplier but provide different quantities to its members. If such differentiation is not feasible, efficiency may require that the international organisation provides the common minimum to all its members, while the remainder is supplied by smaller groups of countries or the individual member-states.

Development Aid Diversity in EU Countries

Development aid may be such a case. But the development aid of the European Union does not meet the above-mentioned requirements. As has been shown, the distribution of bilateral aid is not very similar among the European member-states – both with regard to the recipient countries and, even more so, with regard to the sectors receiving aid. There are much more homogeneous groups of donors than the European Union. The heterogeneity of donor preferences among the European member-states is probably because many of them have been colonial powers. Colonial ties play a more important rôle in the distribution of European aid and aid-financed export orders than they do in the World Bank. This goes back to the origins of the European development aid policy; it was introduced because of French insistence and as a mechanism for redistributing income from Germany to France. In spite of the differences in preferences, decisions about European development aid are not taken unanimously. Moreover, to the extent that the aid is financed from the Community budget, contributions cannot be tailored to the individual donor's preferences.

Money Supply and Currency Competition

The supply and use of money seems to yield considerable economies of scale. Information cost, transaction cost and risk are lower if a common currency is used. However, competition

[31]

among suppliers of money promotes price level stability, and to the extent that real exchange rates have to be adjusted in response to differential shocks, monetary policy preferences are likely to differ on a geographical basis. As in all other lines of production, the only safe procedure for finding out whether money is a natural monopoly good is to remove all barriers to the choice among currencies and to wait and see whether currency competition destroys itself. This is not to deny that individual choice among currencies may generate transaction cost externalities with other users. In competitive markets, however, the external transaction cost varies in proportion with the 'internal' transaction cost that is borne by the individual decision-maker. Thus, the currency that minimises his monetary transaction costs will also minimise social monetary transaction costs. Moreover, externalities never justify barriers to entry. The insistence on barriers to currency competition has to be explained in political rather than economic terms.

A European Income Insurance Mechanism

Advantages of scale have also been claimed for a *European income insurance mechanism.* Some authors advocate automatic transfers among the member-states as insurance against asymmetric shocks to income.[12] There is agreement that insurance is not required for transitory shocks which are later offset. Such cyclical risks are better covered by borrowing in the world capital market. But if the shocks have permanent income effects and if taxpayers are risk-averse, some form of insurance can be efficient provided that moral hazard and the cost of administration are not too large. The decision to insure, however, does not have to be collectivised at the level of the member-states, nor does the insurance itself have to be provided by the Union. Since individuals differ with regard to risk aversion, the decision whether, how much and with whom to insure ought to be left to the individual. The moral hazard emanating from social welfare payments may justify that the government prescribes a minimum insurance cover, but

---

[12] These ideas go back to the so-called McDougall Report (*Study Group on the Rôle of Public Finance in European Integration,* Brussels: Commission of the European Communities, 1977).

private insurances must be eligible as well, and they must be free to diversify on an international basis.

A Common Market May Not Be Enough

The foregoing criteria and applications give a more precise meaning to the concept of subsidiarity. At the same time, they leave some room for judgement.

The analysis shows that a European Union need not be limited to a common market. From a classical liberal perspective, international institutions should also enforce the rules of competition among governments as well as compensation for international externalities (property rights). Whether such a system is called a confederation or market-preserving competitive federalism is probably more a matter of semantics.

At the same time, however, the analysis leaves no doubt that the European Union has obtained a number of competencies which, under an efficient division of labour, belong to the member-states, lower levels of government or individual citizens. These policy failures have to be explained.

III. EXPLANATIONS

Historical experience shows that federal states tend to centralise on a secular basis.[1] In the public finance literature, this tendency is known as 'Popitz's Law'.[2] The USA, Germany, Switzerland, Austria and Australia are well-known examples. After the Second World War, it is true, centralisation was temporarily reversed – primarily because military expenditure declined. But in most countries the share of central government in total government expenditure did not fall to pre-war levels. More recently, from 1972-74 to 1984-86, the share of central government rose from 64·1 to 67·1 per cent in the United States, from 60·2 to 63·6 per cent in the Federal Republic of Germany, from 51·0 to 56·4 per cent in Switzerland, from 72·7 to 76·1 per cent in Austria, and from 75·4 to 77·6 per cent in Australia.[3] Among the federal states, the only notable exception is Canada which shows a secular trend of decentralisation. The Canadian example refutes the view that the technological revolution in transport and communications or the growth of the welfare state necessitated centralisation in the modern age. As we shall see, the experience of Canada can be well explained by its political institutions. An institutional theory of centralisation is required. From it, predictions and recommendations for the European Union can be derived.

---

[1] For a recent discussion of this point, see Clint Bolick, *European Federalism: Lessons from America*, IEA Occasional Paper No.93, London: Institute of Economic Affairs, 1994.

[2] Johannes Popitz (1884-1945) was a German professor of fiscal law who served as state secretary in the Ministry of Finance and as minister without portfolio during the Weimar Republic. He argued that federal states tend to centralise over time; he attributed this tendency to technical progress and increasing preferences for redistribution.

[3] These figures refer to consolidated central government expenditure plus lending minus repayments including transfers to other levels of government and social security. They have been computed from the Government Finance Statistics of the International Monetary Fund.

In the past, the founders of federal states have paid little attention to the dynamics of creeping centralisation. The late William Riker, in his classic study on federalism, draws the following lesson:

> 'As men engaged in expanding a government, they [the writers of federal constitutions] are much more likely to be preoccupied with practical expedients for the moment than with provisions for the distant and not clearly foreseen future. As centralisers, they are much more concerned with centralisation itself than with fears that centralisation may go too far.'[4]

A good example is James Madison, the father of the second constitution of the United States, which in 1789 replaced the less centralist Articles of Confederation. He predicted in his Federalist Paper No.45:

> 'The number of individuals employed under the Constitution of the United States will be much smaller than the number employed under the particular states.'[5]

Two hundred years later, the personnel of the US federal government exceeds the personnel of all the states combined. Thomas Jefferson warned:

> 'I see...with the deepest affliction the rapid strides with which the federal branch of our government is advancing towards the usurpation of all the rights reserved to the States, and the consolidation in itself of all powers, foreign and domestic; and that, too, by constructions which, if legitimate, leave no limits to their power.'[6]

James Buchanan describes the outcome:

> '...it is mockery to use "federalism" or "federal union" in descriptive reference to the United States of 1990, which is, of course, simply a very large nation state.'[7]

---

[4] William H. Riker, *Federalism: Origin, Operation, Maintenance*, New Haven, Conn., and London: Yale University Press, 1964, p.14.

[5] In I. Kramnick (ed.), *The Federalist Papers*, Harmondsworth, Middlesex: Penguin Books, 1987, p.291.

[6] Letter, 1825, in M.D. Peterson (ed.), *Thomas Jefferson. Writings*, New York: Literary Classics of the United States, 1984, p.1,509.

[7] James M. Buchanan, 'Europe's Constitutional Opportunity', in *Europe's Constitutional Future*, IEA Readings No.33, London: Institute of Economic Affairs, 1990, p.6.

The Actors

he political dynamics of centralisation are to be explained, the interests of the political actors have to be analysed. Which actors are interested in political centralisation, and why? We shall apply the theory of public choice and assume that politicians, bureaucrats and even judges are interested, *inter alia*, in power and prestige. Since they have less influence over their income, and are subject to less control, than ordinary suppliers in a market, power and prestige are more important in explaining their behaviour than is usually the case. Very often, the pursuit of power and prestige is subconscious and hidden behind lofty ideals. But it is the major driving force uniting the members of a political institution, especially if their background is highly diverse.

In the European Union, centralisation enhances the power and usually the prestige of the Union institutions proper – the European Commission, the European Parliament and the European Court of Justice.

The European Commission

In public-choice terminology, the European Commission is a bureaucracy. However, unlike national bureaucracies, it is not confined to administration. It is also part of the legislative process. It has the monopoly of initiative for any legislative proposal, and it also proposes the legal basis which determines the required majority in the Council. Any alteration of a Commission proposal (including the proposed legal basis) requires a unanimous vote in the Council. Moreover, unlike national bureaucracies, it is entitled to bring cases before the supreme court of the Union, the European Court of Justice. As one American observer has remarked:

'[I]t is unimaginable that Americans would grant such political power as the Commission staff enjoys to a career bureaucracy.'[8]

Since 1960, the Commission's staff has increased about tenfold, and relative to the Community's population it has more than quadrupled. A control problem is indicated by the fact that after-tax salaries are considerably higher in the

---

[8] Douglas E. Rosenthal, 'Competition Policy', in Gary C. Hufbauer (ed.), *Europe 1992. An American Perspective*, Washington DC: The Brookings Institution, 1993, p.303.

Commission than in the national administrations. For example, they exceed the net salaries of comparable civil servants in German federal ministries by 72-89 per cent. The excess over comparable national after-tax salaries is larger at the European Commission than at the OECD (39-76 per cent) or the IMF (64 per cent on average). The last recruitment competition attracted 55,000 applications for 400 vacancies. The EC Commissioners who, at the time of their appointment, enjoyed the highest political status in their home country, tend to come from member-countries whose central government budget is small relative to the EC budget.[9] This is consistent with Popitz's hypothesis that politicians and bureaucrats are attracted by the government which has the largest budget at its disposal. In 1995, the EC budget (ECU 77,200 million) will exceed the national central government budget of at least nine of the 15 member-states.

Whereas, in the member-states, the bureaucracies (ministries) are controlled by elected politicians (the cabinet), the Commission's administration is not supervised by the Council of Ministers. The Commissioners, it is true, tend to be politicians and are proposed by the member-governments but they are not supposed to take orders from them. They decide by simple majority. They may even pass certain regulations. No voting records are published. The lack of transparency of decision-making is aggravated by an extensive committee system ('committology') in which representatives of the member-states and interest groups participate. At present, there are 376 Commission committees.

The European Parliament

The European Parliament, like most union parliaments, shares the vested interest in political centralisation. It does not control but reinforces the Commission's centralising tendencies. The most visible sign of this bias is the Parliament's almost invariable demands for a larger Union budget than the Council has proposed. While the member-states unanimously determine the total resources of the Union institutions, the Council's budget proposal for the spending of these resources can be overridden by the Parliament with a

---

[9] See my econometric analysis in 'The Political Economy of Centralisation and the European Community', *op. cit.*, Table 5.

qualified majority of 60 per cent. Since the Parliament can only control the non-mandatory expenditures (notably the structural fund, development aid and new policies), it is particularly eager to increase their share in the budget.

In a vote on a spending project, the decisive deputy is likely to represent a lower income group than the decisive Council member does in a qualified majority vote. (A qualified majority in the Council amounts to 71·1 per cent.) This may explain why spending decisions are more easily passed by the Parliament than by the Council.

The median member of the European Parliament is closer to the median member of the Commission than to the decisive member of the Council. This contributes to explaining why, under the co-decision procedure in 1987-89, amendments proposed by the European Parliament have been more often adopted by the Commission (63 per cent on a first reading, 49 per cent on a second reading) than by the Council (41 per cent on a first reading, 22 per cent on a second reading). On an ideological basis, the median member of the European Parliament has been significantly left of the median voter in the Council. As has been shown, this would also be true if the elections for the European Parliament gave the same weight to each vote. These findings relate to the year 1991.

The European Court of Justice

The judges of a federal court increase their discretionary power by expanding the power of the federal government. The more powerful the federal government, the more important the issues which the federal court may decide. It is well known that the Supreme Court of the United States has played a crucial rôle in the process of US centralisation – especially in the early years (under Chief Justice Marshall),[10] in the 'New Deal' era and in the 1960s. In particular, it

---

[10] Thomas Jefferson was one of the first to be worried by the centralising tendencies of the Court. He complained: 'The judiciary of the United States is the subtle corps of sappers and miners constantly working under ground to undermine the foundations of our confederated fabric. They are construing our constitution from co-ordination of a general and special government to a general and supreme one alone. This will lay all things at their feet, and they are too well versed in English law to forget the maxim "*Boni judicis est ampliare jurisdictionem*".' (Letter, 1820, in M.D. Peterson (ed.), *Thomas Jefferson. Writings, op. cit.*, p.1,446.)

reinterpreted the 'interstate commerce clause', 'the power to coin money' and the 'general welfare clause' of the American constitution so as to extend the power of the federal government. Australia is another federal state in which the Constitutional Court has supported centralisation. In Germany, the Constitutional Court, with one exception, has simply let centralisation run its course.

By contrast, the secular decentralisation of Canada is frequently attributed to the fact that, until 1949, the final constitutional court of appeal was not the Canadian Supreme Court but the Judicial Committee of the Privy Council in London. The law lords had no interest in the centralisation of Canada – rather the contrary. The committee enhanced the constitutional status and the legislative sphere of the provinces by interpreting the 'property and civil rights' clause of the British North America Act (1867) in their favour (including the whole field of social legislation), and by severely restricting federal authority under the 'peace, order and good government' clause, the 'trade and commerce' power and the residuary clause.

There is general agreement that the European Court of Justice has acted as an 'engine' of both market and political integration. It has favoured an extensive interpretation of the Community's powers and a 'hands-off' policy *vis-à-vis* the expansionary exercise of these powers by Community institutions.[11] It has developed a number of doctrines not contained in the Treaty – most notably the doctrine of 'pre-emption' (1964) which gives Community law priority over national law (including large parts of national constitutional law).[12] The Court has acted to defend its powers against the

---

[11] Joseph Weiler suggests that 'in its entire history, there is not one case, to my knowledge, where the Court struck down a Council or Commission measure on grounds of Community lack of competence', and he warns that 'no core activity of state function could be seen any longer as still constitutionally immune from Community action'. (J. Weiler, 'The Transformation of Europe', *Yale Law Journal*, Vol.100, 1991, pp.2,446 f.)

[12] 'There is no express provision in the Community Treaties ... for the primacy of Community law over Member State law ... The primacy of Community law is a principle developed by the Court ... Community law prevails even over the Member State constitutions (case 11/70) so that ... the humblest Community provision prevails over the highest Member State law.' (F.G. Jacobs, K.L. Karst, 'The Federal Legal Order: The USA and Europe Compared. A Juridical

new court of the European Economic Area, and it has promoted the establishment of a European Court of First Instance (1987) which handles the less interesting routine cases (competition law and personnel). During the early 1990s, 450 cases were brought before both courts each year, and the average waiting time exceeded two years.

Most cases reach the European Court by way of a preliminary reference from courts in the member-states (Art.177), usually lower-level courts. For these lower courts, the option of referring a case to the European Court is highly attractive because it enlarges their room for discretion and protects them against the superior national courts. To some extent, it even enables them to initiate judicial review over the executive and legislative branches and to enter areas that had been reserved to the highest national courts.[13]

The European Court enjoys considerably more power than national constitutional courts because its decisions interpreting the Treaty can be reversed only by changing the Treaty which requires unanimity among the governments and ratification by all national parliaments. Moreover, the Court's decisions interpreting ordinary Community legislation can be altered only at the suggestion of the Commission and by unanimous or qualified majority decision of the Council. Enlargement strengthens the position of the Court because the difficulty of reaching consensus in the Council increases as the number of members grows.

Each judge is independent except that he might not be re-appointed by his government at the end of his six-year term. Hitherto, re-appointment has been the rule: by 1992, 16 of the 27 judges who were eligible for re-appointment had been re-appointed at least once. The re-appointment ratio is higher for judges (59 per cent) than for Commissioners (40 per

---

Perspective', in M. Capelletti, M. Seccombe, J. Weiler (eds.), *Integration Through Law. Europe and the American Federal Experience*, Berlin, New York: de Gruyter, 1986, p.233.) With respect to some parts of constitutional law, the German Constitutional Court has challenged the European Court's doctrine of supremacy.

[13] For details see Joseph H.H. Weiler, 'Journey to an Unknown Destination: A Retrospective and Prospective of the European Court of Justice in the Arena of Political Integration', in Simon Bulmer and Andrew Scott (eds.), *Economic and Political Integration in Europe. Internal Dynamics and Global Context*, Oxford, and Cambridge, Mass.: Blackwell, 1994, pp.135-39.

cent). Of the 45 judges, 31 have had political or administrative experience. Only four of the 13 judges who were members of the European Court of Justice in 1994 have been judges in their home country before their appointment to the European Court. The European judges are not political neuters.

The European Council

Centralisation or collusion may not only be favoured by the institutions of the Union. Under certain conditions, they are also in the interest of the lower-level governments. In the European Union, these governments are represented in the European Council or, at the level of ministers, in the European Council of Ministers. However, many decisions in the Council of Ministers are not taken by the ministers but by their representatives – national civil servants.

Council meetings in Brussels may provide publicity and prestige, but qualified or even simple majority decisions and the transfer of competencies to the Union restrict the freedom of discretion, and *prima facie* reduce the power, of the national politicians and bureaucrats. Why do they agree to such transfers of power? Several explanations have been offered.

- *First*, by combining together, all members of the Council can enhance or preserve their power *vis-à-vis* the governments of non-member-states. As a European cartel of politicians, they have a stronger bargaining position at the world level.

- *Second*, a European cartel of politicians can be useful in quelling criticism and resistance at home. If all member-governments act in unison, parliamentarians, journalists and voters at home are less likely to raise their 'voice' in protest, and 'exit' is more costly for the citizens. Taxation, regulation, import protection and monetary policy seem to be cases in point. More generally, the Union can serve as an alibi or scapegoat for policies desired by the individual member-governments but not by the median voter at home. Decision-making at the Union level is remote and less transparent, and since the division of power between the union and the national governments is blurred as well ('co-operative federalism'), national politicians can shirk their responsibility. They can hide most easily behind

Council decisions if the latter are taken by simple or qualified majority and if the voting record of the Council and its individual members is not published. (Since December 1993, it may be disclosed.) The governments of the member-states are also attracted by the possibility of delegating to the Union those interventions which they consider necessary to gain or maintain the support of some crucial interest groups but which are unpopular with most other members of their ruling coalition. This contributes to explaining why the European Union has come to specialise in the provision of subsidies, regulations and import protection. It has collected those competencies which the member-governments consider unattractive – their 'dirty work', so to say.

- *Third,* the European Union enables the member-governments to evade parliamentary control. The European Parliament, it is true, has to be consulted in the legislative process, and there are now about 20 types of bills and treaties for which its assent is required. However, its powers fall far short of those of a normal parliament. The bulk of Union legislation is neither controlled by the European Parliament nor by the national parliaments. Directives adopted by the Council must even be implemented by the national parliaments (or the national governments). Whoever used to believe that democratic governments are controlled by parliament must recognise that, in the European Union, the member-governments, assembled in Council, control their parliaments. The European Union serves the interests of the executive branch of government ('executive federalism'). This may help to explain why, say, the Treaty of Maastricht has been more popular among the politicians in government than with national parliaments and the electorate at large.

- *Fourth,* the national politicians tend to give away the powers of lower-level governments and independent public institutions (the judiciary, an independent central bank, the monopoly and mergers commission and other independent regulatory agencies) if they can obtain something else for themselves in exchange. They have an incentive to engage in log-rolling at the expense of third

[42]

parties. Moreover, in the case of autonomous national institutions, centralisation at the European level cannot be criticised on the ground that the Union suffers from a democratic deficit.

- *Fifth* and finally, for many politicians and civil servants the Commission is an interesting career option. Fifty-eight of the 82 Commissioners who have been appointed since 1958 have been cabinet members or civil servants in their home country before they went to Brussels. National politicians and civil servants who are attracted by this prospect may be biased in favour of European centralisation. Diplomats in particular are interested in international harmony and co-operation rather than in international policy competition.

Special Interest Groups

According to a long-standing view that goes back to James Madison,[14] centralisation weakens the influence of pressure groups because, in a larger state, they tend to block each other. Unfortunately, this is true only for special interests confined to the local or national level. It does not hold for groups that share common interests throughout the Union. On the contrary, centralisation increases their influence because they save transaction costs by lobbying one instead of 15 governments and because centralisation raises the cost of political information for the individual consumer and taxpayer who has to pay the bill.

In the case of the European Union, centralisation offers special interest groups the additional advantage that they can lobby a bureaucracy (the European Commission) rather than elected politicians and that the politicians, assembled in Council, are not subject to ordinary democratic control. Owing to the multi-cultural and multi-lingual nature of the Community, they do not even face common media or a critical European public opinion. As we know from the theory of public choice, direct democracy (by referendum) is the most effective way of curbing the influence of pressure groups. But the European Union is close to the other extreme. This may explain why, in most member-countries, support for the Maastricht Treaty has been stronger among business

---

[14] See *Federalist Paper* No.10, in I. Kramnick (ed.), *The Federalist Papers, op. cit.*

associations than among voters. Within interest groups, the lobbyists at the union level have the strongest incentive to advocate a centralisation of policies.

Since 1955, the number of European pressure-group organisations has risen more than ninefold. According to one source,[15] there are almost 3,000 lobby organisations and 10,000 lobbyists in Brussels. Madison proved to be wrong – in both the United States and Europe.

Three Kinds of Favours

The favours to interest groups take three forms: protectionism, subsidies and regulation. It is well-known that the external trade policy of the European Union is highly protectionist – especially its so-called 'anti-dumping' measures and 'voluntary' export restraints. As for subsidies, at least 72 per cent of the Union budget is spent on favours to interest groups. The bulk goes to agriculture, and the Treaty of Maastricht has added a Union competence for industrial policy. The extent of EC regulation cannot easily be quantified. One author has simply counted the pages in the *Official Journal*. He reports that 78 per cent of the legislation was devoted to special interest groups.[16] There can be no doubt that the European Union is more strongly affected by lobbying than any of the member-states.[17]

Regulations Confer Rents

Most regulations are designed to confer rents on pressure groups. In other words, they raise the profits of producers by directly or indirectly restricting output. They limit entry, reduce competition and harm the consumer. Since they interfere with freedom of contract, they tend to cause larger welfare losses than do subsidies. But for politicians and bureaucrats, regulation is highly attractive because its budgetary cost is low and its redistributive effects are not

---

[15] G. Naets, 'Lobbying in the European Community', *Business Journal*, February 1990, pp.20 f.

[16] William S. Peirce, 'Unanimous Decisions in a Redistributive Context: the Council of Ministers of the European Communities', in R. Vaubel and Th.D. Willett (eds.), *The Political Economy of International Organisations*, Boulder, CO.: Westview Press, 1991, Table 2.

[17] This is also the conclusion drawn by S.S. Andersen and K.A. Eliassen, 'European Community Lobbying', *European Journal of Political Research*, Vol.20, 1991, p.178.

transparent. This is especially true for the European Commission which lacks the power to increase its revenue or to issue debt, and which can shift the cost of enforcing the European regulations onto the member-states. For the Council, too, it is easier to introduce new regulations than to grant additional subsidies. A new regulation may be introduced by qualified majority, whereas an increase in the budget requires unanimity among the governments and consent of the parliaments of the member-states. Interest groups are particularly keen on regulations and protection because barriers to entry are the only way of securing permanent gains. They also prefer environmental standards to pollution charges, which may explain why the common environmental policy is entirely based on standards.

In the literature on rent-seeking, there is some debate whether bureaucrats or politicians are more accommodating in their dealings with interest groups. This debate is relevant to the European Union because, for the reasons mentioned, the Commission enjoys more power *vis-à-vis* the Council than national bureaucracies do *vis-à-vis* their governments. Some authors have argued[18] that bureaucrats are more forthcoming than politicians because, unlike the latter, they do not face a re-election constraint. Politicians, by contrast, must fear to lose votes from consumers and taxpayers whenever they supply regulations and subsidies to organised interest groups. Bureaucrats may also be more accommodating because they are more likely to be hired by the industry they have been regulating. The demands from interest groups are welcome to the bureaucracy because they contribute to the growth of its power. Sometimes, the Commission even encourages interest groups to lobby with Council members.

The matter is different, however, if an interest group – say, a farmers' association – can offer a potentially decisive block of votes to politicians. While bureaucrats are relatively more responsive to rent-seeking from capital-intensive industries like the steel or the motor industry, politicians may be more responsive to rent-seeking from labour-intensive sectors such as agriculture. But even in these cases, the Community is more

---

[18] See, notably, W. Mark Crain, Robert E. McCormick, 'Regulators as Interest Groups', in J.M. Buchanan and G. Tullock (eds.), *The Theory of Public Choice – II*, Ann Arbor: University of Michigan Press, 1984, pp 287-304.

accommodating than a national government would be because the Council is much farther removed from the attention and control of the media and the voters. The introduction of the Common Agricultural Policy, for example, has raised the average level of agricultural support prices in every member-country.

European regulations are not only easier to come by. In several respects, they are also more valuable to special interest groups. If Union regulations are substituted for national regulations, European producers tend to improve their competitive position *vis-à-vis* producers in the rest of the world because they can exploit economies of scale in production, design the common standards so as to ward off competition from abroad, and improve the bargaining position of their commercial policy-makers in international trade negotiations.

Quest for EU Regulation

The quest for Union regulation is partly a defensive reaction to increasing market integration under the Internal Market Programme and to the principle of mutual recognition of national regulations which the European Court of Justice had established in its Dassonville and Cassis de Dijon decisions. Both market integration and mutual recognition were bound to erode the regulatory power of national governments and the influence of interest groups. The European Court had been the most likely European institution to introduce mutual recognition because it is least accessible to European interest groups. Moreover, in its rulings, the court granted itself broad discretion as to which national regulations do not have to be recognised.

As has been pointed out in the juridical literature, the Single European Act has enabled the Community executive and European interest groups to contain the far-reaching implications of mutual recognition (Art.100 B) and to facilitate EC regulation by departing from the unanimity principle (Art.100 A).

Under the qualified majority requirement of Art.100 B, mutual recognition is fairly improbable, and has not been agreed upon so far, because the least regulated 71 per cent of the member-states are not interested in deregulatory competition towards the level of the least regulated member-state. Instead, under Art. 100 A, the most highly regulated 71 per cent may introduce Union regulations which are at least as restrictive as the national regulations of the least re[...] member-state belonging to the qualified majority co[...] Moreover, as the deregulatory pressure on the coali[...] reduced by these minimum Union standards, each member of the coalition will raise his national level of regulation, and this rise will again be imposed on the Union minority (and so forth). Current and past experience with the Single European Act seems to be consistent with these public-choice considerations.

In certain circumstances, it is true, a member-state may continue to apply its national regulations despite harmonisation (Art.100 A (4)). But this option is available only if the national regulation is more restrictive than the Union regulation. Thus, the escape clause is asymmetric and biased in favour of regulation.

Raising Rivals' Costs

The Social Chapter of Maastricht extends qualified majority voting to social regulation. Once more, it enables the interest groups and governments of the highly-regulated member-states to extend their own regulations to the other member-states. In industrial economics, this is called 'the strategy of raising rivals' costs'. It is a standard explanation of regulation. Several American authors have argued[19] that, for example, federal minimum wage legislation and the Occupational Safety and Health Act (OSHA) in the United States have served the North to suppress competition from low-cost labour in the South. In Germany, the Social Chapter as well as the Social Charter have been advocated by both the trade union congress and the employers' association. The British government has opted out instead of vetoing the Social Chapter. This, too, is a policy of raising rivals' costs.[20] Other areas of application are taxation, environmental standards, competition policy and vocational training. In all these

---

[19] For example, George Stigler, *op. cit.*, p.2, and T. Heller, 'Legal Theory and the Political Economy of American Federalism', in M. Capelletti, M. Seccombe, J. Weiler (eds.), *Integration Through Law. Europe and the American Federal Experience*, *op. cit.*, pp.271 f., 277.

[20] However, it is likely to be short-sighted. If and when Britain ratifies the Social Chapter under a government more sympathetic to labour unions, regulation will become more severe than it would have been with British participation and the unanimity principle.

spheres, the interest groups of the highly taxed and regulated member-countries try to raise their rivals' costs towards their own level.

Social regulation, too, is a response to trade liberalisation and increasing competition in the Union. The strategy of raising rivals' costs rests on two necessary conditions which are likely to be satisfied. *First,* labour mobility among the member-countries must be low so that rising unemployment in the less-regulated countries does not depress wages in the highly regulated countries. *Second,* the additional unemployment in the less-regulated countries must not be financed entirely by the more prosperous, highly regulated countries, or it must be financed by the general taxpayer rather than the special interest groups in these countries.

More difficult to explain is the adoption of the Social Chapter by governments of the less-regulated member-states (except Britain) which must have known that they would be outvoted by more-regulated member-states and that their level of social regulation would rise both absolutely and in relation to the other states. Why did they abandon their earlier national regulatory equilibrium?

Benefits of Maastricht's 'Cohesion Fund'

The first possibility is that the governments of the less-regulated member-states received something else in exchange: larger transfers due to the Maastricht 'cohesion fund', the prospect of sharing control over European monetary policy, the new industrial policy and the extension of qualified majority voting to various EC policies other than social policy.

The British opt-out from the Social Chapter could then be explained by the British government's expectation that it would not reap net benefits from monetary union, industrial policy, the extension of majority voting and, of course, the cohesion fund.

But there is also an explanation that does not rely on log-rolling or issue linkage. Completion of the internal market may have raised the level of regulation desired by trade unions and median voters in the less-regulated member-countries because the removal of barriers to capital movements between member-states has increased the demand for labour in the labour-abundant low-income countries. This increase in the demand for labour has raised the rent-maximising return to labour and, as part of it, the equilibrium level of social regulation in these countries. Since, at the same time, demand in the national labour markets – but not in the European Union as a whole – has become more cost elastic, interest groups increasingly prefer European to national regulation.[21]

The theory of rent-seeking can also explain why some interest groups have been more successful than others in obtaining European regulations, subsidies and protection. Farmers, for example, have not only benefited from their voting potential and the union-wide homogeneity of their products but also from the low price elasticity of demand for their products and the self-contained nature of agriculture which limits the spillover of rents to other sectors.

Voters

Centralisation, even where it is inefficient, may be in the interest of a majority of voters if it redistributes income and wealth in their favour. In the European Union, there are no union-wide referenda, and the redistributive powers of the European Parliament are fairly limited. But a large number of redistributive measures passes the Council – many of them by qualified majority (71 per cent).

Since the member-governments rarely represent much more than 50 per cent of their voters, a qualified majority in the Council is not likely to represent more than 40 per cent of the voters of the Union. This is due to the cumulation of two majority decisions, one at the national and the other at the European level. Majority voting at the constituency level (as in Britain and France) lowers the required percentage even further. In the Union of Fifteen, a qualified majority decision in the Council requires 62 out of 87 votes. The voting weights of the large member-states are smaller than their population shares. If we ignore the constituency effect and simply assume that each member-government represents 50 per cent of the country's voters plus one, and if, for example, the qualified majority decision is taken against the United Kingdom (10

---

[21] For further details and a diagrammatic exposition see my article 'Social Regulation and Market Integration: A Critique and Public Choice Analysis of the Social Chapter', *Aussenwirtschaft / The Swiss Review of International Economic Relations*, No.1, 1995.

votes), Germany (10 votes) and the Netherlands (5 votes), the qualified majority of the Council represents no more than 29·2 per cent of the voters of the Union. The problem has been aggravated by the fact that the Community, which initially consisted of three large and three small countries, has subsequently been joined by more smaller than larger countries.

To what extent can centralisation be explained by the interests of voters if, in the Council, each government is assumed to represent the interests of its median voter at home?

If member-states are ranked by their net *per capita* payments or receipts *vis-à-vis* the European Union, France was the decisive voter in the Council in the second half of the 1980s. As public choice theory would predict, France was close to breaking even but, by the end of the decade, it had slipped slightly into the red. The two major net contributors are Germany and Britain. (The three new entrants from among the EFTA countries will be net contributors as well.) Since the decisive voter can (and is likely to) veto systematic redistribution at his expense, it was an important issue how the qualified majority rule would be redefined for the enlarged Union. It has been decided that, in the last resort, the percentage will stay at 71 per cent. This means that the casting vote will go to a major net contributor, probably Austria. She is likely to alter the pattern of redistribution until she breaks even or gains.

Support for EU from Countries Which Benefit

A multiple regression analysis of opinion poll data for the Union of Twelve[22] reveals that popular support for European unification is significantly stronger in countries which receive net payments from the Union budget and have a low GDP *per capita*. However, the simple correlation between net receipts and GDP *per capita* is negative because those members which have the highest incomes (Denmark, Luxembourg, Belgium) are net recipients. Thus, overall redistribution among the member-states is regressive. The structural funds are an exception. This may explain the strong negative correlation

---

[22] Roland Vaubel, 'The Political Economy of Centralisation and the European Community', *op. cit.*, Table 10.

between the member-countries' GDP *per capita* and popular support for the centralisation of social policy.[23]

Net payments from or to the Union budget are only a rough and incomplete measure of redistribution. Some payments (for example, to Belgium and Luxembourg) are not transfers but payments for services even though the bulk of the Union budget is spent on subsidies rather than union-wide public goods. Moreover, there are problems in allocating tariff revenue to individual member-states. Finally, much of the redistribution is implicit rather than explicit. For example, voters who supply factors of production in the capital of the Union or in other cities or regions hosting major Union institutions benefit from centralisation (as long as congestion is not a serious problem). That is why, in the United States, citizens of the District of Columbia are not entitled to vote in Congressional elections. European centralisation is also likely to be favoured by the electorates of those member-states which have the least satisfactory system of government.

Opinion surveys reveal that voters are less enthusiastic about European centralisation than their governments and parliaments. Responsibility of the Union is rejected by a majority of voters for several policy areas which the Union has entered – notably education, health and social security, workers' security, cultural policy and the media.

The Dynamics of Creeping Centralisation

From the interests of the various actors the equilibrium degree of centralisation can be derived. But this is merely a static (game-theoretic) equilibrium. Additional considerations are required to explain a self-driven, dynamic process of centralisation. Is it true that 'centralisation breeds further centralisation' as, for example, Sam Beer has argued?[24]

Jean Monnet believed that the process of European integration would be propelled by 'spillovers' between markets and corresponding linkages between policy areas. For example, market and policy integration with regard to coal and steel would spill over into manufacturing, from there into agriculture, and so on. In similar vein, Jacques Delors has

---

[23] The correlation coefficient (r) is 0·48.

[24] Sam Beer, 'The Modernization of American Federalism', *Publius* (The Journal of Federalism), Vol.3, No.2, 1973, p.52.

claimed that the internal market requires, *inter alia*, an approximation or centralisation of regulations, a social dimension, a common policy on mergers, a common currency, union control of national budgetary policies, and subsidies for trans-European networks. As we have seen, several of these arguments are invalid or at least insufficient to justify what has been done. But they seem to have played some rôle in persuading the general public.

The issue linkages which have driven the process of centralisation have rarely been of the sort that the removal of one distortion required the removal of distortions elsewhere (as is assumed in the theory of the second-best). Usually, the issues were not linked by allocative but by distributional considerations. Each step of market liberalisation was accompanied by complaints from some partners that they would not get a fair share of the gains from market integration and that some new common policies had to be added to redress the balance.

When the European Economic Community was founded in 1957, the French government claimed that the common market for manufactures would benefit Germany rather than France; in exchange, it insisted on common policies for agriculture, development aid and nuclear energy. When Britain joined the Community as a major net contributor, the British Labour Government insisted on the creation of a European Fund for Regional Development (1975) to reduce the British burden, even though the Community probably lacks a comparative advantage in selecting suitable projects at the regional level. (In the meantime, the Commission's autonomy in allocating resources under the common regional policy has even been enlarged.) When the Single European Act was negotiated, the 'poor-four' (Spain, Portugal, Greece and Ireland) secured a doubling in real terms of the structural funds. In the negotiations about the European Economic Area and the Treaty of Maastricht, they obtained two 'cohesion funds' which will subsidise specific expenditures in their countries.

Many of these package deals rest on dubious assumptions about the distribution of the welfare gains from market integration.[25] However, much more serious from an economic

---

[25] According to classical allocation theory, the main beneficiaries from market integration have been the small and central member-economies – that is, the

point of view, they have become a means of centralising policies for which the Union does not have a comparative advantage. If distribution effects of market integration are to be offset, side payments (cash transfers) are the efficient solution. But the governments of the contributing member-countries prefer implicit transfers to explicit payments, possibly because they want to conceal the cost and the interest-group orientation of their policies from their voters. Even if voters in the contributing countries preferred in-kind transfers to cash transfers, they would probably not wish to give in-kind transfers which are inconsistent with an efficient division of competencies.

Expanding the Budget Reinforces Centralising Tendencies

There is a second dynamic of centralisation. Any expansion of the Union budget and the Union institutions alters the way in which the political system responds to changes in the demand for the services of the Union institutions. The larger the resources at the disposal of the Union, the more it will be able to support centralising demands and to counteract decentralising forces. For the same reason, it is easier to found a new institution than to abolish it. Even if demand for the services of the Union fluctuates symmetrically around a constant mean, this response asymmetry generates a secular process of centralisation.[26]

The most extreme form of a response asymmetry is a ratchet effect. As we have seen, several institutional features of the European Union act as ratchets. *First*, the Commission's monopoly of initiative ensures that centralising measures are not easily reversed. *Second*, if the Commission is opposed to an amendment, the Council may only adopt it unanimously. *Finally*, since most decisions of the Council require unanimity or a qualified majority, the Council cannot easily modify the

---

Benelux countries. These countries have been net recipients of funds from the Union budget. The poorer members are peripheral countries but their economies are small. Within these countries, the factor labour has greatly benefited from free trade, capital movements and migration. However, the structural and cohesion funds of the Union are largely used for the benefit of labour in these countries.

[26] For a formal exposition see my article 'The Political Economy of Centralisation and the European Community', *op. cit.*, p.158.

decisions of the European Court of Justice which decides by simple majority.

The ratchet view of political integration is also firmly established in the strategies and rhetoric of the union institutions. Already the Preamble to the EEC Treaty declared 'ever closer union' to be the aim. Later on, the Community developed the doctrine of the '*acquis communautaire*' which is now enshrined in the Treaty of Maastricht (Art.B). The *acquis communautaire* must never be questioned – either in negotiations with new members or in applying the principle of subsidiarity. At a more popular level, the Commission propagates the so-called 'bicycle theory of integration': if political integration does not advance, it will falter.

Passing Thresholds Towards Centralisation

Centralisation is likely to accelerate when certain thresholds are passed. A first threshold is reached when the union budget or personnel is equal to the budget or personnel of the central government in a majority of member-countries. With the recent enlargement, the European Union has passed this budget threshold. Since politicians and bureaucrats are attracted by the larger budget, the passing of the threshold triggers a natural selection effect and the most competitive politicians and bureaucrats turn to the Union government. This strengthens the Union institutions and weakens the member-governments.

Of course, the natural selection effect does not have to be modelled as a discrete threshold effect. If the Union is attractive for other reasons, for example because it offers the highest net salaries, politicians and bureaucrats may want to join the Union institutions even though the Union budget is still smaller than the central government budget of their home country. In these circumstances, the brain drain to the Union increases as the Union budget approaches the size of the central government budget of the home country even if it does not reach the threshold, and the natural selection effect is best captured by a continuous variable, say, the ratio between the two budgets. My econometric analysis supports this interpretation.[27]

---

[27] R. Vaubel, 'The Political Economy of Centralisation and the European Community', *op. cit.*, Table 5.

Another threshold is passed when the resources of the Union government exceed those of all member-governments combined. At this point, centralisation can become irreversible. In the United States, this threshold has been passed for both the budget and personnel.

IV. PROPOSALS

In the classical liberal literature on European constitutional reform, two major approaches can be distinguished. The first group of authors starts by determining the ideal division of labour between the Union and its members. It applies the theoretical criteria of Section II and possibly proceeds to inquire how the optimal assignment could be stabilised. This will be called the conceptual approach. It is typical of the German literature. The alternative approach is to take the European *status quo* as the starting point and to reform the procedures of Union decision-making in such a way that the Union will gradually evolve in the direction of subsidiarity. This is the procedural approach. It is more widespread among Anglo-Saxon writers.

The Conceptual Approach

Classical liberals who use the conceptual approach re-invent the Union from scratch. They design a European (con-) federation or minimal state whose powers are exhaustively enumerated and strictly limited. New powers may either not be added at all or only under very restrictive conditions.

According to the analysis of Section II, such a Union would have few competencies:

- It would be given the exclusive responsibility to ensure the free movement of goods, services, capital and labour within the Union.

- It could prevent the member-governments from granting subsidies, imposing regulations or pursuing procurement policies which discriminate against foreign suppliers. Its surveillance of public procurement would cover government purchases of both inputs and final public goods and services to be provided to the general public.

- It could control mergers, and proceed against cartels, of companies from different member-states, and it would act as a court of appeal in all other matters of competition policy which cannot be covered by the WTO (successor to GATT), the OECD or some other more comprehensive

[56]

organisation. In this subsidiary rôle, the Union would not be permitted to be less strict than the national competition authorities.

- It would be responsible for the enforcement of environmental and other compensation agreements and property rights among member-states. Co-operation in the field of environmental policy would be confined to transnational pollution.

- It would be given exclusive responsibility for trade policy *vis-à-vis* non-members but it would not be permitted to erect new trade barriers.

- If the Union had a common defence and foreign policy, it would only address matters which the other members of the Atlantic Alliance did not wish to take up. The Union would not need troops of its own for this purpose.

Since the powers of the Union would be strictly limited, many liberal adherents of the conceptual approach would be willing to accept simple-majority decisions in most of these fields. The most likely exceptions are foreign policy, defence and environmental protection (within the above-mentioned constitutional limits), because preferences may differ considerably in these spheres. The larger the damage which a potential minority would suffer, the more important is unanimity. The high income differentials among the member-states do not permit low majority decisions.

The conceptual approach is useful insofar as it points the direction and offers an inspiring vision for the future. However, as the history of the United States, Germany, Switzerland and other federal states has shown, exhaustive enumeration of very limited powers is not sufficient to prevent a secular process of centralisation. Moreover, the conceptual approach does not tell us how we can bridge the gap between the current state of the Union and the liberal ideal.

The Procedural Approach

From a present-day perspective, the most promising starting-point is the principle of subsidiarity enshrined in the Treaty of Maastricht (Art.3 B). It is true that the formulation of the principle in the Treaty leaves much to be desired. It presupposes, for example, that any treaty objective which cannot be sufficiently achieved by the individual member-states can 'therefore' be better achieved by the Union. But it shifts the burden of proof to the Union institutions and confines them to actions which are necessary to achieve the objectives that can be better achieved by the Union.

At the summits of Birmingham and Edinburgh (1992), much care was taken to clarify the legal meaning of this article. However, the main problem remains unsolved: the application of those legal terms to real-world cases. Like most theological terms, 'subsidiarity' leaves much room for interpretation. The crucial question is who is going to interpret it.

Under current procedures, the decision rests with the Commission and the Council, to some minor extent with the European Parliament, and ultimately with the European Court of Justice. As we have seen in Section III, the Commission, the Parliament and the Court have a vested interest in centralisation. The principle of subsidiarity, by contrast, requires that, in case of doubt, the responsibility must be assigned to the member-states. We have also seen that the Council is not a reliable judge because the national politicians may wish to use the Union to reduce the electoral cost of catering for interest groups, to collude against their voters and to evade parliamentary control. Subsidiarity, therefore, can be interpreted only by the national parliamentarians or the voters themselves. This implies that the problem of subsidiarity and the democratic deficit of the Union are intricately linked: subsidiarity will not prevail unless the democratic deficit is closed.

Control by a Chamber of Delegates of the Member-Parliaments

The weakest and least direct method of giving national parliamentarians control over Union legislation is to establish a second chamber of the European Parliament consisting of delegates of the parliaments of the member-states. This has been proposed by the European Constitutional Group[1] (of which I am a member). Each deputy of the second chamber

---

[1] Peter Bernholz *et al.*, *A Proposal for a European Constitution*, London: European Policy Forum, December 1993. There have been reports that, at the Intergovernmental Conference of 1991, the French government, too, suggested establishing a Senate made up of national parliamentarians.

would at the same time be a member of the parliament of his home country and be selected by it. He or she would serve for no more than five years and could be recalled by the national parliament at any time.[2] The second chamber would have the right to review and possibly amend all legislative proposals to ensure that the principle of subsidiarity is respected.

The proposed chamber is reminiscent of the old European Parliament as it existed up to 1979. The fact that, in that year, delegation was given up in favour of direct election points to the political vulnerability of the scheme. Once more, we may also recall the experience of the United States. Under the Articles of Confederation, Congress consisted of delegates elected by the state legislatures (one from each state). The Constitution of 1789 added a directly elected House of Representatives and transformed the old Congress into a Senate whose members were still elected by the state legislatures, now two for each state. Finally, in 1913, the Seventeenth Amendment introduced the direct election of Senators because delegation was considered undemocratic. There were also charges that it had led to corruption. When the Senators initially refused to agree to the change, they were threatened with a constitutional convention that would curtail their powers. The second European chamber would probably not be quite so vulnerable because, with the same weights, direct election would make it a mere duplicate of the first chamber. However, at the time of transition, a different weighting scheme might be introduced for the second chamber so as to distinguish it from the first chamber. As we know, a US-type Senate is not an effective barrier to centralisation.

The proposal to add a chamber of delegates points in the right direction but the study of constitutional history raises doubts that such delegation would be durable. Moreover, it is a less direct form of democratic control than one would wish, and it would attract the most centralist members of the national parliaments to the second European chamber.

Control by the Parliaments of the Member-States

These problems can be avoided if national parliaments themselves participate in the legislative process of the

---

[2] Term limitation and the possibility of recall were also characteristic of the US Congress under the Articles of Confederation.

:opean Union. At present, the rôle of the national rliaments in European legislation is not defined by the Treaty, and very different arrangements prevail in the various member-states. In each member-state, parliament has to ratify amendments to the Treaty and all major international treaties of the Union. It also has to implement the directives of the Council. But it is only in Denmark, Britain and the Netherlands that parliament effectively tries to control the way the government votes on directives and regulations in the Council.

In Denmark, parliament has set up a committee for relations with the Union which not only has the right to receive information about the proposals of the Commission but can, and at times does, oblige the government to oppose them in the Council. However, the obligation is not of a formal nature, nor are formal votes taken in the Committee.

In the United Kingdom, the Select Committee on European Secondary Legislation can involve the House of Commons before decisions are taken in the Council. The Committee itself has the right to receive, and comment upon, the draft proposals of the Commission. Moreover, if the Committee recommends such a proposal for consideration by the House, the government may not vote for it in the Council before the House has considered it unless the Minister concerned decides that, for special reasons, agreement should not be withheld. However, it is extremely rare that the House holds a formal vote of approval or disapproval on these matters, and even a Commission proposal that has been disapproved by the House may in principle be accepted by the government in the Council.

In Germany, the Bundestag and its European Committee do not even have a delaying power over ordinary Union legislation. However, a recent amendment of the constitution (Art.23 *Grundgesetz*) and a recent decision by the German Constitutional Court (October 1993) have strengthened the rôle of parliament in other respects:

- Union legislation which implies or requires changes of the German constitution has to be adopted with a two-thirds majority of both houses.

- Union legislation which primarily affects the competencies of the German Laender (provinces) has to be adopted by the second chamber (Bundesrat) consisting of delegates of the Laender governments.

- Germany may not enter the third stage of European Monetary Union without the assent of the Bundestag.

Subsidiarity Requires National Parliaments' Control

There is certainly no case for Union control over national parliamentary procedures. But if subsidiarity is to prevail, the Union Treaty must give national parliaments control over Union legislation. The procedures could be the same as for national legislation. In policy areas which do not fall within the Union's exclusive competence, all Union directives and regulations would have to be submitted to the parliaments of the member-states. In areas for which the Treaty requires unanimity, the parliaments of all member-states would have to agree by simple majority. Where the Treaty requires a qualified majority, the parliaments of a qualified majority of the member-states would have to agree by simple majority. Thus, agreement by a member-state would require the assent of its government (in the Council) and its parliament. Ideally, national parliaments would not delegate their final decision to a specialised parliamentary committee because the members of such a committee could easily develop an interest of their own.

The interest of the national parliaments, it is true, tends to be biased against the centralisation of powers at the Union level. But the same bias is implicit in the principle of subsidiarity. Thus, in case of doubt, the lower-level governments and parliaments ought to decide. The present stock of Community legislation consists of about 1,700 directives and about 24,000 regulations. The proposed procedure would act as a check on the sheer quantity of new Union legislation and on its centralist bias. It would force the Union to concentrate on the provision of a liberal economic order rather than *ad hoc* interventions and discretionary policies. The proposal to integrate the parliaments of the member-states into the legislative process of the Union is, no doubt, unusual and far-reaching. But since the traditional bicameral systems have proved incapable of preventing secular centralisation in almost all federal states, an institutional innovation is clearly inevitable.

In those areas which fall within the Union's exclusive competence, legislation would not be submitted to the parliaments of the member-states but to the European Parliament.

Control by the Voters

Interest groups find parliamentarians less accessible than are cabinet members and bureaucrats; the influence of pressure groups declines with the size of parliament.[3] But the deputies of the governing party or parties are biased in favour of the government because they want to be promoted by it. To the extent that they are not elected in a constituency but from a party list they even depend on the party leadership for their re-election. Moreover, voters seem to dislike disunited parties. For all these reasons, the most effective protection against rent-seeking and undesirable centralisation is direct democracy by referendum. But there is a trade-off because voters, owing to their number, have little incentive to inform themselves and face considerable information and transactions costs. As a consequence, only very important and simple issues are suitable for referenda.

One such issue is the overall size of the Union budget. The European Constitutional Group has suggested[4] that any increase of the Union budget relative to the Union's GNP would require not merely the current procedure for treaty amendments but also direct approval by a majority of voters in the Union and in a majority of the member-states that are net contributors to the Union budget. There may even be a case for requiring a popular majority in all member-states that are net contributors.

An alternative which has been suggested elsewhere[5] is to finance all Union expenditure from a single proportional

---

[3] See, for example, R.E. McCormick, R.D. Tollison, *Politicians, Legislation, and the Economy*, Boston: Martinus Nijhoff, 1981.

[4] P. Bernholz *et al.*, *op. cit.*, Tab 2 a, p.8; Tab 2 c, p.12; Tab 2 a, Art.XXI, Sections 6 and 7.

[5] Bernholz, 'Constitutional Aspects of the European Integration', in S. Borner and H. Grubel (eds.), *The European Community after 1992. Perspectives from the Outside*, London: Macmillan, 1992, pp.45-60; Friedrich Schneider, 'The Federal and Fiscal Structures of Representative and Direct Democracies as Models for a

income tax or a value-added tax and to require a referendum whenever the proportional tax rate is to be raised.[6] This implies that the Union would not be permitted to issue debt. Expenditure increases within the tax limits might require unanimity in the Council. At the very least, those member-states which are net contributors to the Union budget would have to keep their right of veto.

Vertical Competition

Maximum competition among politicians or bureaucrats requires that the division of powers between the Union and the member-states can be adjusted. Europe needs not only horizontal but also vertical competition among governments. But who is to decide about such transfers of constitutional competencies between higher- and lower-level governments?

In the European Union, the decision is partly left to the Union institutions. According to Art.235, the Council may unanimously adopt all appropriate measures that are necessary to attain, in the course of the operation of the single market, one of the objectives of the Community, provided that the Council is acting on a proposal of the Commission and after consulting the European Parliament. The decision of the Council is subject to review by the European Court of Justice, and, in several cases, the Court has preferred a more specific legal basis. But the general empowering clause of Art.235 has been widely used. At present, more than 30 measures are based on it. Obviously, vertical competition cannot be unbiased if the institutions of the Union are free to decide which instruments are appropriate and necessary to attain the general objectives of the Treaty. Art.235 has to be eliminated.

In Germany, the constitution enumerates the competencies of the federal government exhaustively. Amendments of the constitution require a two-thirds majority in both houses. Since the Second World War, there have been more than 20 transfers of competencies from the Laender to the federal government but only two in the reverse direction. Usually, the

---

European Federal Union: Some Ideas Using the Public-Choice Approach', *Journal des Economistes et des Etudes Humaines*, Vol.3, 1992, pp.403-37.

[6] This is essentially the Swiss régime. The Swiss constitution (Art. 41 ter) sets upper limits for the federal turnover and income tax. Thus, the limits cannot be raised without a constitutional amendment which requires a popular referendum. There are also cantonal income taxes.

Laender governments in the Bundesrat are bought off with federal money, or they prefer joint legislation with the first chamber to control by their Laender parliaments. The first chamber, by contrast, tends to veto proposals for devolution. As German experience shows, the parliament of the Union must not be able to control the constitutional assignment of competencies between the member-states and itself.

In the United States, Article V of the Constitution gives the states ultimate control over the constitution. Not only Congress but also the legislatures of two-thirds of the states can initiate a constitutional convention, and the amendments proposed by the constitutional convention have to be ratified not by Congress but by the legislatures or conventions of three-fourths of the states. But the states did not use their constitutional power to check the process of centralisation. They were bought off with federal grants, or each of them may have feared that a constitutional convention might get out of control and propose amendments it disliked. In the same way, the problem of agenda control might deter the member-states of the European Union from calling intergovernmental conferences when they are concerned about the increasing power of Union institutions. Adjustments in the assignment of competencies must not require constitutional conventions or intergovernmental conferences. The parliaments of the member-states must be able to amend the Treaty by consecutive voting.

In Switzerland and Australia, the constitution is amended by popular referendum. In both countries, a majority of voters in the Union and in a majority of the provinces has to assent. The Federal Constitution of Austria (Art.44) prescribes a referendum for any total – that is, fundamental – revision of the constitution (such as the abolition of the provinces); but any other constitutional amendment only need be so submitted on the demand of one-third of the members of either chamber.[7] Unlike the governments of the German Laender and unlike the legislatures of the US states, Swiss, Austrian and Australian voters cannot be lured by federal money (which they have paid themselves in taxes). But

---

[7] There are also non-federal member-states whose constitutions provide for constitutional referenda. If the constitution is to be amended, a referendum is mandatory in Denmark and Ireland, and it is optional in France, Italy and Spain.

Switzerland, Austria and Australia have been centralising as well. This is probably because the median income tends to be lower than the arithmetic mean income so that the median voter gains from an increase in public goods and services even if it is financed from proportional rather than progressive taxation.

Centralisation and Redistribution

Centralisation facilitates redistribution. It cannot be contained in a direct democracy unless centralising constitutional amendments which increase the scope for redistribution require qualified majorities.

The experience of Switzerland and Austria suggests that the threat of referenda induces the politicians to form broad coalitions as a counterweight. This 'consensual' or 'consociational' style of government implies that the politicians have to make their decisions unanimously or by qualified majority. But since they share an interest in centralising political power, this safeguard is not sufficient. The qualified majority rule has to be applied to the referenda as well.

Another constraint on constitutional amendment which could usefully be applied to check centralisation, is contained in the constitutions of Belgium (Art. 131), the Netherlands (Art.137), Luxembourg (Art.114), Denmark (Art.88) and Sweden: if the chamber of deputies wishes to amend the constitution, it has to dissolve itself, call an election, and vote again.

If subsidiarity is to prevail, the voters of each member-state must also be free to decide in favour of partial opt-outs (by simple majority) or in favour of secession (say, by qualified majority). To maintain transparency, it might be useful to confine the opt-out option to policy areas rather than specific measures. The Schengen Accord and the Treaty of Maastricht have established the principle. The formal right of secession is an important check against the suppression of minorities. The secular process of decentralisation in Canada is frequently attributed to the credible threat of secession by Quebec.

The Canadian Constitution Act of 1982 even introduced a formal right of opt-out. Art.38 reads as follows:

'An amendment...that derogates from the legislative powers, the proprietary rights or any other rights or privileges of the legislature or government of a province...shall not have effect in a province the legislative assembly of which has expressed its dissent thereto by resolution supported by a majority of its members prior to the issue of the proclamation...'.

Can Britain become the Quebec of Europe?

In the United States, by contrast, the Civil War removed the threat of secession once and for all and thereby paved the way for the ensuing centralisation. The European Constitutional Group suggests that states which have voted in favour of opt-outs or secession must not be excluded from the common market.[8] Thus, the external trade barriers of the Union could no longer be used to exact political concessions from applicant countries.

Finally, democratic control by the voters of the Union would become more effective if all voting records had to be published and if a single procedure were used for all legislation in which the European Parliament participates. Responsibility requires transparent procedures of decision-making and a clear delimitation of powers.

Control by a European Constitutional Court

Since the European Court of Justice has a vested interest in European centralisation, it must not have the final say on subsidiarity. Otherwise, the experience of the United States and Australia might easily be repeated.

One approach is to reform the European Court itself. For example, it is probably desirable to limit the number of terms a European judge may serve. If re-appointment is a matter of routine (as it used to be), term limitation might make a difference because the prospect of having to return to his home country might curb the centralist inclinations of a Union judge.

This effect would fail to materialise, however, in the case of older judges whose (last) term ends with retirement.

Another, complementary approach is to change the rôle which the European Court plays in the European legal system. First of all, the power to refer cases to the European Court could be confined to the highest courts of the member-states (or the courts of last instance). This would help to reduce the

---

[8] P. Bernholz *et al.*, *op. cit.*, Tab 2 c, p.5; Tab 3 a, Art.XXX, Section 4.

excessive workload of, and waiting time at, the European Court. It would also prevent the lower courts from bypassing higher courts and thereby improve the consistency of jurisdiction in the member-states.

Second, it has been suggested by the European Constitutional Group that, just as a second chamber consisting of delegates of the national parliaments might be added to the European Parliament, the European Court of Justice could be complemented with a Court of Review which would be empanelled, at the suggestion of the individual member-states, from judges serving on their highest judicial authority.[9] This Court of Review could be viewed as a constitutional court but it would be responsible only for cases which, in its view, require an interpretation of subsidiarity. All other cases would continue to be handled by the full-time judges of the European Court of Justice, including its Court of First Instance. Since the judges of the Court of Review would remain members of their national courts, they would be less likely to be biased in favour of centralisation at the Union level. To prevent such a bias from developing, the European Constitutional Group suggests that no judge may be delegated for more than eight years.

Control Through Asymmetric Decision Rules

The decision rule which most effectively protects subsidiarity is unanimity. From the Luxembourg compromise (1966) to the Single European Act (1986), the Community operated essentially on this principle. The SEA introduced qualified majority voting on the Internal Market Programme, and the Treaty of Maastricht has extended it to various other policies (including several which, according to the conceptual approach, ought not to be centralised).

In political theory, the unanimity rule serves as a bulwark against the suppression of minorities. Since the utility which different individuals derive from some specific political action cannot be measured, let alone be compared or aggregated, the only way of assuring that the change is an improvement is to require the consent of all those concerned. Hence, (quasi-) unanimity is indispensable at the constitutional level. The

---

[9] Bernholz *et al., op. cit.,* Tab 2 a, p.9; Tab 2 c, p.9; Tab 3 a, Art.XV.

transfer of powers to a government can be legitimised only by consent.

But what about the withdrawal of such powers? As Wicksell pointed out,[10] by the logic of this argument, the withdrawal of powers does not require (quasi-)unanimity. On the contrary, even if only a significant minority withdraws its approval, the government has lost its legitimation to use these powers. Thus, the decision rule must be asymmetrical depending on whether powers are given to, or withdrawn from, government.[11] In the context of the European Union, this has two important implications.

First, if the Union is to introduce regulations, taxes or barriers to trade and factor movements, unanimity must be required in the Council because the Union desires powers which infringe upon the freedom of the individual. For the same reason, qualified majorities should be required in the European Parliament and in European referenda. Yet if, as in the Internal Market Programme, barriers to trade and factor movements are removed and a competitive lowering of regulations and taxation is encouraged, a simple majority or even a qualified minority would be sufficient.[12] In the case of legislation which is neither restrictive nor liberalising, the quorum would have to be somewhere in between.

Second, by the same principle, the transfer of powers from the member-states to the Union requires the assent of all governments and parliaments of the member-states and of a qualified majority of the voters, but only a simple majority or even a qualified minority would be sufficient for a repatriation of powers (for example, in agricultural policy).

The classical liberal cannot approve of symmetric decision rules. Liberalism implies an asymmetry in favour of individual freedom and political decentralisation.

---

[10] Knut Wicksell, *A New Principle of Just Taxation* (1896), in R.T. Musgrave and A.T. Peacock (eds.), *Classics in the Theory of Public Finance*, New York: St. Martin's Press, 1967, pp.72-118.

[11] This point is also made by the European Constitutional Group (Bernholz *et al.*, *op. cit.*, Tab 2 a, p.6; Tab 2 b, p.5).

[12] In the context of the last GATT round, the asymmetry has been reversed: the Council will require a qualified rather than a simple majority to block anti-dumping and other protectionist measures proposed by the Commission.

The institutions of the European Union do not only require more effective control from outside. The division of labour among them should also be reformed. The present rôle of the Commission is, for example, inconsistent with the separation of powers.[13] The Commission must become a professional civil service.

1. The Commission should not be the legislative agenda setter. The separation of powers requires that it should not have a right of legislative initiative at all. The right of initiative should be reserved for parliaments (say, a qualified minority of the European or the national parliaments) and those elected by them (say, a qualified minority of the Council).

2. The Commission's rôle in the legislative review process is also inconsistent with the separation of powers. The required majority in the Council must not depend on the vote of the Commission.

3. The separation of powers requires that the Commission should not have (quasi-)judicial functions. For example, anti-cartel and anti-merger proceedings and anti-dumping investigations are better left to an independent and non-political competition authority.

4. As a civil service, the European Commission must not have the right to bring cases before the supreme court of the Union, the European Court of Justice. If the European Commission was transformed into an ordinary administration, it would only be entitled to suggest court action to the Council, the chief executive body.

5. Like any civil service, the Commission should be supervised by an elected executive, the Council of Ministers, in all its administrative functions. A body like the Council whose

---

[13] The liberal principle of the separation of powers is due to John Locke (*Second Treatise of Government*, 1690), and Charles Montesquieu (*The Spirit of the Laws*, Book VI, Ch.VI, 1748). Montesquieu distinguishes the executive, the legislative and the judicial branches of government.

composition changes slowly and whose President is chosen by rotation is also better able to evolve the consensual framework of rules which a group of highly heterogeneous countries requires. The President and the other members of the Commission, by contrast, serve contemporaneous five-year terms.[14]

6. To avoid a centralising brain-drain, net salaries at the Commission should not be higher on average than the net salaries for comparable positions in the national civil services. If, at the same time, the pecuniary incentive to join the Commission is to be the same for the civil servants of all member-states, Commission officials must be paid the same after-tax salary as the equivalent grade of civil servant in their country of origin (with due adjustment for any differences in purchasing power). This is the 'origin principle'. It is used to determine the salaries of the members of the European Parliament.

The procedural reforms proposed in this Section are not required only to preserve a decentralised order of decision-making in Western Europe. They would also help to prevent the Union from abusing the powers it should have. For this purpose, it is not sufficient to copy the control procedures that exist in the member-states. The Union institutions must be subject to more stringent control than the governments of the member-states because individual preferences are more heterogeneous, and external constraints (exit and voice) are weaker, the larger and less open a society is. As several econometric analyses have shown,[15] openness has a significant negative effect on corporatism, the share of government transfers in GDP, and the rate of inflation.

---

[14] *Cf.* Frank Vibert, *A Non-Coercive Union – The Constitution for Europe*, London: European Policy Forum, 1995, Ch.8.

[15] *Cf.* Pierre Salmon, 'Checks and Balances and International Openness', in Albert Breton *et al.* (eds.), *The Competitive State*, Dordrecht: Kluwer, 1991, p.179; David Romer, *Openness and Inflation: Theory and Evidence*, Cambridge, Mass.: National Bureau of Economic Research, Working Paper No.3936, 1991.

V. THE OUTLOOK

The intergovernmental conference of 1996 offers a welcome opportunity to implement procedural reforms which would move the Union in the direction of subsidiarity. Now that the subsidiarity principle has been enshrined in the Treaty, the next step is to give effect to it. There is a chance that, in hindsight, the Treaty of Maastricht will prove to have been a turning point. The reasons are as follows:

First, the Treaty has provoked a fundamental debate about the past and future course of European political integration, setting a learning process in motion. Academics, journalists and many voters have come to understand that what seemed to start as a purely economic undertaking is really meant to attain political objectives, and that political decision-making at the European level is too important to be left to the specialists (most of whom are fervent advocates of European centralisation). The process of self-selection has been disturbed. Most important, in several (mostly major) countries, politicians have learnt that European centralisation can be a vote loser.

Second, as the Community is increasingly moving into the field of political integration, its problems of legitimacy abound. As long as it focussed on market integration (the liberalisation of trade, capital movements and migration) it could draw its legitimation from individual liberty. Subsidiarity was not endangered but promoted. The centralisation of policy, however, cannot be justified in this way: quite the contrary. Its legitimation – if at all – can derive only from democracy. But the Union lacks democratic legitimacy.

Third, as the Internal Market is completed, the gains from market integration are exhausted among the existing members. In the absence of further enlargements, they will not reap further gains from specialisation which they can redistribute through additional common policies. Moreover, the cost of German unification will prevent Germany from continuing to serve as the 'paymaster of Europe'. Policy centralisation by redistributive issue linkage simply cannot go on.

Fourth, the accession of Sweden, Finland and Austria will increase the diversity of preferences in the Union. As in the case of Britain and Denmark, peripheral members and latecomers tend to be less enthusiastic about European centralisation than the founding members. That is why they join later. However, as the history of the United States has shown, enlargement of the Union by additional states is not sufficient to stop centralisation. It merely slows it down. It will even increase the weight of the Commission *vis-à-vis* the Council because a rigid bureaucracy which decides by simple majority is in a better position to digest diversity than occasional meetings of national politicians who have to find a consensus. Enlargement does not render constitutional reform unnecessary.

Fifth, there is a widespread perception that transformation of the East European countries is the main challenge which Europe has to meet in the near future and that, from both a political and an economic point of view, full integration with the European Union is by far the best response. The need to accommodate these countries might act as a brake on European centralisation and redistribution and require the repatriation of powers (such as agricultural policy).

Sixth, the military threat from the East has diminished, if not disappeared. This has profound implications for members like Germany which turned to the European Community as the second pillar of their security policy when France withdrew from the military organisation of NATO. Germany may not need European political union for its security any longer – not because of German unification but because the Federal Republic has ceased to be a frontier state. This change in Germany's interests should not be mistaken for nationalism. It supports the forces of democratic decentralisation and the peaceful competitive order which freedom requires.

Nevertheless, there remain serious causes for concern. European Union institutions have a vested interest in continuing on the path of creeping centralisation. Commission, Court and Parliament may be willing to stave off pressure for the time being and be content to make fuller use of the new competencies they have gained. But they will resume their quest for ever more powers when the time seems ripe. The governments of the member-states are interested preserving a system which enables them to evade parliamentary control. Under the cover of the traditional foreign policy prerogative, they have succeeded in taking over from their parliaments a large part of what used to be domestic legislation. The democratic deficit, after all, is not a coincidence. There are powerful actors who benefit from it. *The only effective cure is institutional and procedural reform. The initiative has to come from the parliaments of the member-states.*

QUESTIONS FOR DISCUSSION

1. Why is centralisation a threat to individual freedom?

2. What distinguishes the classical liberal from the nationalist?

3. Do international differences with regard to taxation, subsidies and regulation distort the allocation of resources?

4. Which international non-market externalities are of more than bilateral importance but confined to the European Union?

5. Can transfers among the member-states be justified as an efficient insurance mechanism?

6. Why do federal states tend to centralise on a secular basis?

7. Why is the European Union more susceptible to lobbying than any of the member-states?

8. Why have the Cassis de Dijon judgement and the Internal Market programme increased the pressure for Union regulations?

9. Is the 'democratic deficit' an obstacle to subsidiarity? If it is, how can it best be overcome?

10. Can the centralisation of powers be checked by constitutional means? If so, how?

11. Why is the rôle of the Commission inconsistent with the separation of powers?

FURTHER READING

Addison, J.T., and S.W. Siebert, *Social Engineering in the European Community: The Social Charter, Maastricht and Beyond*, Current Controversies No.6, London: Institute of Economic Affairs, 1993.

Andersen, S.S., and K.A. Eliassen, 'European Community Lobbying', *European Journal of Political Research*, Vol.20, 1991, pp.173-87.

Aranson, P.H., 'The European Economic Community: Lessons from America', *Journal des Economistes et des Etudes Humaines*, Vol.1, 1990, pp.473-96.

Bernholz, P., 'Constitutional Aspects of the European Integration', in S. Borner, H. Grubel (eds.), *The European Community After 1992. Perspectives From the Outside*, London: Macmillan, 1992, pp.45-60.

Bernholz, P. *et al.*, *A Proposal For a European Constitution. Report by the European Constitutional Group*, London: European Policy Forum, 1993.

Peirce, W.S., 'After 1992: The European Community and the Redistribution of Rents', *Kyklos*, Vol.44, 1991, pp.521-36.

Rasmussen, H., *On Law and Policy in the European Court of Justice*, Dordrecht: Nijhoff, 1986.

Schmieding, H., *Europe After Maastricht*, Occasional Paper No.91, London: Institute of Economic Affairs, 1993.

Shapiro, M., 'The European Court of Justice', in A.M. Sbraghia (ed.), *Euro-Politics*, Washington: The Brookings Institution, 1992, pp.123-56.

Vaubel, R., 'Currency Competition and European Monetary Integration', *The Economic Journal*, Vol.100, No.402, 1990, pp.936-46.

Vaubel, R., 'The Political Economy of Centralisation and the European Community', *Public Choice*, Vol.81, 1994, pp.151-90.

Vibert, F., *A Non-Coercive Union – The Constitution For Europe*, London: European Policy Forum, 1995.

European Federalism: Lessons from America
CLINT BOLICK

1. Decisions in Europe about federalism will determine '...not only whether the Continent's inhabitants are prosperous and competitive, but whether they are free'.

2. 'Federalism' is largely an American invention. But the word is used in very different senses, sometimes meaning centralisation and sometimes meaning decentralisation.

3. The founding fathers of the US Constitution saw federalism as a means of diffusing and dispersing government powers to preserve individual liberties.

4. However, despite constitutional safeguards, there has been in the USA a 'tremendous accretion of central power and a concomitant loss of constituent state government power and individual freedom'.

5. Europe should draw lessons from US experience of federalism: in particular, it should beware of centralising tendencies.

6. The subsidiarity principle - 'far less specific than the subsidiarity principle embodied in the Tenth Amendment to the US Constitution' - is inadequate as a protector of economic liberties.

7. Britain should insist on four essential safeguards before entering a federal enterprise in Europe. The first is that federal powers are 'carefully defined and limited' and that no other federal power is exercised except with unanimous approval.

8. A right of secession, to make subsidiarity meaningful, is the second safeguard.

9. The third safeguard is a constitutional guarantee of 'essential liberties' against infringement.

10. Finally, and particularly important, a federal Europe would need a 'truly independent, life-tenured judiciary' with power to invalidate federal government actions, and 'legal standing should be conferred upon individual citizens'.

ISBN 0-255 36336-2   IEA Occasional Paper No.93

IEA

The Institute of Economic Affairs
2 Lord North Street, Westminster
London SW1P 3LB
Telephone: 071-799 3745

£5.00 inc. p.+p.

ECONOMIC AFFAIRS

The journal of the IEA

Spring 1995

Financial Regulation issue

(edited by Professor Harold Rose)

Main Articles

Harold Rose	Introduction
George Benston	'The Sins of Banking Regulation in the USA'
David Llewellyn	'Regulation of Retail Investment Services'
Maureen O'Hara	'Derivatives: What's Needed to Protect the Financial Markets?'
Donald Brash	'Banking Supervision: New Zealand Adopts a New Approach'
Harold Rose	'Financial Regulation - The Underlying Issues'
Jim Stretton	'Regulating Life Assurance: Objectives and Machinery'

Individual issue £2.50

Annual subscriptions:

UK & Europe: £15.00 (Institution); £10.00 (Individual);
Rest of the World: £20.00/$35.00 (Surface); £30.00/$50.00 (Air)

Please apply to:

**The Institute of Economic Affairs
2 Lord North Street, Westminster
London SW1P 3LB**
Telephone: 0171-799 3745: Fax: 0171-799 2137

The Minimum Wage:
No Way to Help the Poor
DEEPAK LAL

1. Controversy among economists about the effects of a minimum wage has recently been revived.

2. Recent studies apparently support the views of politicians in the United States, Britain and other European countries who would like to set or increase minimum wages.

3. These studies claim that minimum wages can increase both employment and the efficiency of the economy.

4. The claim rests on the assumption that labour markets are monopsonistic (employers have considerable market power). But no evidence is produced that monopsony is widespread.

5. 'Dynamic monopsony' (where workers have imperfect information about job opportunities) is said to be a circumstance in which setting the minimum wage can increase efficiency.

6. However, the label 'monopsony' is misapplied to situations in which employers and employees are searching for ways to adapt to uncertainty: divergences between wages and marginal products are the norm in real-world labour markets.

7. Minimum wages would have widespread effects on labour markets. They would, for example, reduce human capital formation because they would compress the wage structure and undermine incentives to acquire skills.

8. Thus support for a minimum wage is '...at odds with [the] desire to promote skill accumulation by unskilled workers – particularly the young and females'.

9. 'Revisionist' ideas which support minimum wages are an exercise in 'Nirvana economics' in which an 'imperfect' market is implicitly compared with the perfectly competitive ideal.

10. Even if labour markets were 'riddled with monopsony', technocrats could not have the information required to apply corrections: '...there is no obvious technocratic solution which would be better than that discovered by the market'.

ISBN 0-255 36344-3

IEA Occasional Paper No.95

The Institute of Economic Affairs
2 Lord North Street, Westminster
London SW1P 3LB
Telephone: 0171 799 3745
Fax: 0171 799 2137

£4.50 inc. p. + p.

The End of Macro-Economics?

DAVID SIMPSON

1. The distinguishing feature of developed market economies is incessant qualitative change. New consumer and capital goods, and new methods of production and distribution are continuously being created and old ones destroyed.

2. Macro-economics looks at economic activitiy in terms of aggregates and averages. It obscures rather than assists an understanding of the essential features of economic activity in a market economy.

3. Macro-economics makes unwarranted assertions about the stability of empirical relationships between aggregates, assumes their unchanging composition, abstracts from essential elements of economic activity, and uses concepts out of context.

4. It is impossible to predict to what extent an increase in aggregate demand will be reflected in price rises and to what extent in output increases. In order to know what significance to attach to a numerical value for any aggregate, one has to disaggregate.

5. Aggregate concepts such as the NAIRU, the quantity of money, the output gap and competitiveness are all misleading, and have contributed to the implementation of unsuccessful and sometimes harmful policies.

6. Almost 20 years since it was publicly acknowledged that a government could not spend its way out of a recession, it has been discovered that the fine-tuning of bank lending does not work either. In the UK the operation of monetary policy has been uncoupled from macro-economic theory.

7. The cycle is an intrinsic part of the deregulated developed market economy and one cannot have the benefits of growth without it.

8. Repeated surveys have shown the complete failure of all attempts at short-term forecasting using macro-economic models. Only pattern predictions are possible.

9. Macro-economic theory is a dead-end in the history of economic thought. The way forward is to return to the classical tradition which emphasises the importance of uncertainty, innovation, entrepreneurship and institutional evolution, and has quite different policy implications.

10. Policies to approach full employment must facilitate the adaptation of workers from old jobs to new jobs. Taxes should be shifted from employment to consumption and subsidies should shift from unemployment to the search for, and acceptance of, new employment.

ISBN 0-255 36338-9

Hobart Paper 126

£8.00 inc. p.+p.

The Institute of Economic Affairs
2 Lord North Street, Westminster
London SW1P 3LB
Telephone: 071-799 3745

Delta Blues

Skip Fox

*aha*dada

books

tokyo / toronto

General editor: Jesse Glass
Typesetting: Joe Zanghi, Printed Matter Press
Cover photo: Rikki Ducornet

editorial address:

3158 Bentworth Drive
Burlington, Ontario
Canada L7M-1M2

First Edition
Printed and Bound in Canada

ISBN 978-0-9811704-2-8

Some of these pieces earlier appeared, occasionally in different form, in *88*, *Adventures of Max and Maxine*, *Aught*, *Big Bridge*, *Back Box*, *Cricket On-Line Review*, *Exquisite Corpse*, *Dirty Swamp*, *Fell Swoop*, *House Organ*, *Indefinite Space*, *little red leaves*, *The Poet's Corner*, *Real Poetic*, *Sawbuck Poetry*, *Snow Monkey*, *there*, *Unarmed Journal*, *Wheelhouse*, & *Wire Sandwich*.

Delta Blues is the 4th in a series texts tentatively titled *Dream of a Book*. It was preceded by *What Of* (Potes & Poets), *At That* (Ahadada), & *For To* (BlazeVox).

The South is limited yet lacks limits.
–Hui Shih

table of contents

Wrong from the Start

Coffee maker no work, cashed its drawers, closed its stupid eye and died. Bitch. The soft cow that did bid gat me well, that no harm come on me, a ready "Well Met" each morning, that stroked my cheek, pinched my nipple, and drooled sweet drops of words into my ear, melodic, the song's refrain, "Never shall we see the end," has fucking croaked. If I was half the man I used to be, she'd be spread out across the table this very moment. Instead of writing about it, my pinkies would be lubing her inmost gaskets with a gravy-flavored KY, or torturing her "spongy" springs. Greasy Greeley. Really, Creeley? stickas!) No, hardly. I was given tools as toys on my fifth birthday. Living then in Wyoming where everything that happened "turned out," that is, was a direct if not immediate result of something like conscious decision-making, grounded in character, fate, individual though generic, coming vaguely from the land, the meagre soil, which had, I was made to feel, an ineffable but insistent connection to my wee balls. We left when I was seven. I remember roundups of fifty years ago, can nearly smell the burning hide and hair in the fine atmosphere of youth, the far West, on the high plains where you can see the Rockies for a day, almost, driving.) At my last shop, I had a house. In it a wife, and three children, a dog. It all seemed normal, like it had somewhere to go, somewhere from which to have come. A cancelled subscription this morning, 5:32 a.m., dreaming of new ways to make coffee without getting up. In another hour, birdsong and dawn.

"A person, homeless and native" (C. Martin). Severe the abeyances, like pigeons, the city's doves, a blind man's soft hello hello hello into the street, darkness of noon, his face lit, maybe someone you grew up with, you're always looking too closely, as into the faces of buildings (is there a melody beneath?), or the presence of your face greets him like skinned genitalia atop a tossed salad, their reds a sick joke on a bed of greens, . . . and lots of traffic. He hypnotizes himself, makes himself dream that *this* is his life, standing thus, in God's ear, that he is Homer, verily, and the city his tape-recorder, hello hello hello as if to save his place, a map, like holding your thumb, hello hello makes him think that he belongs, and into the city's peace, has been here all his life, is made of words.

Blue Note: A Valentine for the New Millennium
(John Wayne delivery, gruff & bemused)

A kiss is just a kiss
But just remember this,
Every time you kiss her, Bud,
Well . . . you'll be tasting my dick.

Sure Shots

–Sticka for the New Millennium: cone stold sober.

–"The New American Century." As a sticka for what? Dialectical obsessives? Or branding a line of cars? (Chrysler presents *The New American Century*, etc.) Insurance Motto? Program on a late night CNN slot? Anthology/ textbook as cashcow/unbowed-image? The virulent vacuum of such words.

–the heavy, hairy nuts of an aging actress

–"who is it that runs me off the road while jogging, takes pleasure in so doing, shoots at passengers on a train, wants the multitude under his thumb as if it was the state's, say, or are they in the army, behind bars, or in *holy martyr-mony*, . . . whose mouth and mind are clogged with imperative's obscenity from the first sound they ever uttered until now, smothered beneath thoughtless want . . . long live the common man, etc." (Richard LaPauvre)

–Bumpersticker for a New Millennium: Leviticus Be Damned! (It would also work well on a sweatshirt, as Clai Rice said.)

–Self-satisfaction is often the reason I talk to myself. How will that help me be serious? Do I only want to sound serious?

–Calibration exercise, #11: Do you want people to think you are brilliant, or do you want to write poetry?

Sortilege

You will work on a single manuscript in near silence for a years during the course of which you will realize your best work, brilliant and exhilarating. It will be as though you've never read before. After sanding every appositive and polishing each comma, you will send it to the finest English-language literary publisher in the world, a man of profound understanding and exquisite tastes who funds the press out of his rear pocket, stuffed with a staggering fortune in steel. He will be the only person capable of seeing your work for what it is on the first pass. While reading your manuscript one long summer afternoon, "Here it is! Here it is!" will be heard coming, at approximately half-hour intervals, from his second story office, the "at last!" unnecessary, implied in his exclamations' very torque. After each burst, his wife, twenty-four years his junior, lounging by the pool below, will briefly wince and frown from beneath her canted cartwheel. Yet each time, after initial signs of irritation, a secret smile will steal across the shadow of her face as she remembers the soft hands of the assassin, who the next day will climb the staircase sometime between one and two in the afternoon, and do what he was paid to do while she's visiting her sick aunt in Pittsburgh. Occasionally she sets down her shitty romance and dreams of a near future when she may fully indulge her tastes for casinos and young men without fear of discovery. *Her* "at last" is a breeze, nearly articulate, sliding over the upper reaches of her face.

The next afternoon you will be waiting for your new publisher's second call, the first having excited you to "the taproot of [your] being," re-convincing you of life's worth, sustaining your hope humankind, and provisionally staying the unsteady hand of your suicide. The following day as well you will wait by the phone. And the next. The next. All is silent. Adieu.

Sure Shots

–Jay's double hinge or swinging gate. Later, grackles in the bamboo settling in for the night, exactly at sundown, the previous half hour remarkable displays of flight, gathering and spreading in clouds, tier over tier, fandango–life *is* preoccupation with itself, as Olson said–where *their* squeaky gates and swinging doors constitute a grove of birds, more interesting by far than a village crammed with maiden aunts, nuns, and widowers all squawking about squat.

–When have I imagined a self?. . . but one simply, in a chair, or driving, running, sitting at my desk. *Life is preoccupation with itself.* . . . There appear to be many ways of being so occupied.

–Don't put your eggs in *any* basket.
  Eat 'em on the spot, or let 'em rot
  Then throw 'em at someone. ♫

–from a actual testimonial on behalf of cancer research and new drugs: "Ten years ago I might not be sitting here today."

–On rap and social responsibility: Did Homer worry that he might weave a melancholic masculinity into the fabric of our culture? Is Achilles Hamlet? Does Outcast's braggadocio echo the shouts of Hector?

–Black Hole in the Cartesian Box: René, where does all this "I" business come from? All you can truly say is "There is thinking going on, therefore there is thinking going on." One wonders just how much of that.)

T. V. for T. V.'s Sake: Notes for a Polite Essay with two lines by Holly Scullo

That's lots of letters standing up and little words. They wheel the doctor into emergency surgery to remove the knife he planted. Maybe he loses his wit as well, and his wife in a card game. *Television is the imagination*, you're right Holly, and we its eye, looking back on us on ourselves in a chair, long abandoned, in an empty room. We scratch our heads and almost pause but there's too much else to do (that's lots of little words as well): skiing with grandpa, rhubarb pie, the dairy's gone bust and curdles nightly, the holster's lying in the attic beside the dried rat and your collection of business cards, remember? In fact, Americans have the world's longest life expectancy due to the extraordinary amount of nutritious television that they watch daily, not to mention the steroids, adrenaline, antibiotics, and docility inducers they ingest with their animal products. (Maybe if they would lose a bit weight they would live forever.) Also, t.v.'s always there whether one needs it or not, and it's never bitter like roadkill. Only sometimes, late at night . . . Or, even better, television carries us to realms where we are the visitation *and* the place, its vegetation, all clowns *and* circus, a lost eye watching ourselves like never before, furious, our excitations are such, riding the prodigious energies of that stream. Or its flat face slapped up against our genitals has brought us a doubling of our nature, and a doubling of that in *its* nature and due time which is now duplicate and as natural, I suppose, as any bubbling up from the surface of that which pops into current existence. The monstrosity! (Maybe it has always been such.) The tube shines a rare light into the recesses of our rooms which become full and burst with the fragrance liquids tonguing our genitals, our every crevice, column, curve in mind's delight. Each moment the immaculate deception, and we each moment's Joseph. (But we forget the question. Only occasionally remember the answer. Wait a few minutes, it's bound to get better. As Bill asked when I told him Holly's "T.v. for t.v.'s sake": "How else?"

Yesterday a couple of Carolina wrens set up house in the covered grill. I hadn't
closed one smoke-hole.) They probably woke Nancy and Bill who had opened
their window onto the porch the previous evening. Over coffee, they remarked
on its song. This morning, company gone, Jolivet sits patiently at the front door,
becoming the world's most ardent student of Carolina wren behavior. Spring.

The difference between prose and poetry is that prose is horizontal and poetry is
vertical in the same manner that cooking is horizontal and fucking vertical or falling down a man hole, as dreams are as well, unless of course you dream in prose.
Good prose should first and always be good poetry. As anybody knows. A
lake filled with fish. The schoolbus with children, drives off. Azalia blossom.

Each time he walked in the woods, he could hear the life around him duck
for cover. Down by the old plant these were dry sounds. In the pines, soft
like laughter after a good joke. When he came to the pond, the syllables were wet
and broke on his ear like a watery bell, or a seashell. Entranced, he wrote a
score. Once, while conducting his Twentieth, he was lost forever. Birdsong.

In the fact of the face of it, being or essence, ever here's insistence, mugs up
tugging you, reminding you of gravity every moment of every hour except some
nights in dreams . . .) that you are simply a soft swirl in he whose mouth
matters, a squeeze in whose cheek your juice is briefly savored then spit out in an
arc like Earth's final joke, whatever that is, that is . . . what is it? Farm machinery.

Substance itself the permeability by which non-existence crosses from oblivion's
ripeness into being, blossoming of appearance, thing, unfurling of *is* within the
actual, green apparatus of time and place against the dramatic blues and grays this
morning between rains, for instance, in treeline or darkness of clouds is what
anyone could possibly mean by being coming into existence. Cars on the curve.

A turbo beneath empires of leaf, dark whirlings, abeyance of oblivion welling
thru mind of green, existence oozing to skin, galaxies torn asunder, thrown from
roof, with sudden emergence of a single word it's always and only sudden) while
this morning upon every surface entire syllabaries are born, then dance in pearly
florescence and into the sweet ayre of springe. All my life past telling. Treefrog.

Or an edge in sky each evening, a man staked belly up on the beach where a tide is born, then leaves as darkness advances and crabs crawl out of the surf (it's going to be a long night!), or a steer, imperfectly stunned, who *wakes up on the line* under bone-saw and knife, skinned, flayed, evisceration in progress, never knew all these places he could feel those things: knives, nozzles, men. Gecko.

A good dose of cancer might finally teach you something, *une pomme du cerveau,* deep scaring of cranium as question for moment only pitching over falls, for all answer is, but an interrogation like the rocks are fast approaching. But if you're eighteen it's just goddamned unfair. Or if you're thirty-seven. Or eleven. Lives end in early mist. Spring dawn. How lovely the words, like seasons, forgotten.

Perfection is its seed, it sprouts in rose and weed alike, in relations and the dearth of relations, upon the towers of Manhattan, near a mosque in a poor patch of Paris, on a roof in Ecuador or perhaps it's dreaming just outside the room you are in, dreams you are reading as it enters, or is about to knock & change everything, down to your socks. It's just checking your address, thinking. Delicious word.

Imagine a dense black stone, polished like onyx, set in a universe without stars, possibly lacking dimension, total dark, eyes torn from mind, streaming black, unending endedness. Now imagine what *it* might be thinking, that there are places language can't shine its light, nor fill with its bitterness, nor stroke its tiny balls, the sole flaw of existence is appearance, its redemption without words.

The world enters with simple force, pure, as though there were no agency beyond the frame, just volume of sheer appearance, genitals of phenomena shoved in your face, everything has one side, only, and is always here, in this season with more insistence. Radical of presence, exponential, indigenous to an invisible quotient, inarticulate press of existence, time over all the world. Morning call of grackle.

In isolation, blindness without context, mind as new moon, His Royal Absence on Imperial Tour of provinces and far-flung dominions or an old stoner deep into Alzheimer's, . . . how can you tell the difference? Would the universe miss the moon? A man doing handsprings in May? Would isolation be companioned that it be spared the darkest recognition. Nothing need exist. Nothing. Nevertheless.

Word at day's end

the onslaught of bronzed grackles begins
with a few scouts in the cypress,
then the cypress flush in their cacophonies
(what music to what ears?) and
the barn dance begins, clouds of grackles from this tree to
that, when one tree flushes the others are
quiet, briefly . . .
tree to
tree on this three acres,
tier over
tier, cross
cut,
looking up,
you could be swallowed . . .
from tree
to tree, finally circling the
bamboo, then a wave flies in,
and another, and another, 'til it's
filled, this grove, with the caws, mews, soft
screams, clucking as bass, and the thrashings of
wings
against the stuff of bamboo and other wings, perhaps
torsos, before
they flush again and the earth is silent except for someone testing a motorcycle in the distance but
they are soon back, filling the grove (grackles are
vertical) with epics, sorrows, delights, yet no misgivings,
again
flush,
and again return,   this time or the third they
will stay,   the thrashing sounds like a   waterfall in a
small cove, walled-in rock, falling four feet,
six across,
bright   sound of water splashing,   also the feet of

10

a thousand supplicants   at once

    in the sand
           beneath their chanting

   the bright reptilian
        mind
            which

  gradually dies,
       calls softer
           silence more articulate

Sounds in the Sound (predawn grackle grove)

—a bank of frogs deep into spring evening when darkness is nearly complete and you call it the beginning of night and quite often can't remember your name for their lovely barking

—bright mew, cat-slice of sound, only gorgeous, doing intervals

—a wind sound a lost or hollow gush like the passing of something specific and swift, soundless itself, a lost ghost wandering where he left his body

—leafy springs in lovely weather, throat burst, flowers in flame, blossoms on those sleepy hills, vines

—one, a gate hinge that wind keeps pushing in a rhythmic pattern never to be discerned, though thoroughly recognized, opening and closing in its extent, forty minutes til sunrise, I have poured my life into words

—a lost kitty scream of lonely terror, but very high, way down in the mix, or maybe it's an orgasm, or the recitation of a tale begun *long before this*, the *secret history of us*, collective voice of anguish over the mortal condition, the inconsolable extant

—a pewtered twill breaking its silence every seven seconds

—smallest squeezebox of sound hiding like a lantern among trees at night, lost chord of solace finding itself, continually, curious but very certain

—sound as supple crest, slightest fluorescent tip of flame at wave's forward edge, stuttering florets running before the smallest idea of feet, vibrance of dayspring's pinkest (barest) orange

—a kissing, barely audible, but as though kissing were fragile, itself, nearly lost

—deep soft squawk like bearing down with a pestle over a mashed nut, the oils of which coat the mortar's inner surface, partially

–around the perimeters, a series of clucks on pendulums, deep enough to crush boulders, if boulders were to listen, much less attend as closely as the rest, who at the slightest disturbance of its rhythm or tone, quiet, a few flush

not one sound that touches ground

Sentences

You can think of death as a patient friend, but why bother? More likely a fat accident in the original calculation. The death of fathers grace our names as the grace of fathers names our death. Grace dies in father's name. *moms softhearted dads not,* in daughter's notebook, age 9. When you have children, desert yourself. Tie yourself in a corner and pray.

What's Your Sign? A Horoscope for Every Day of the Year
–for Charles Kramer

Aries: The opening of stars, silent and serious, tempered with an understanding that existence is just beginning, and always. The sacred bowl of living shall be yours, overflowing. Earth at cusp of creation. Awe your lot, inspiration, and the lot of your progeny if you fulfill but one bequest: blood sacrifice of every piece-of-shit Pisces you find, . . . after ritual torture.

Taurus: The sun is a bull plowing a furrow through stars. So the fuck what? Your Mars is rising. Success is crest bubbling over crest aloft like the horizon on a tide of good fortune lasting the rest of your life. And beyond. Never to be compromised. Never qualified. If you come upon a Pisces and fail to do him or her great harm, all bets are off.

Gemini: The smallest clouds will touch your hills but only for picturesque and dramatic purposes. Cities will be founded in your honor. Many wise men will come to seek your council. Up a small path kept clear by disciples. In the next room, someone will always be singing your name. With but one requirement, that you pump lead deep into the brain of every fuck-addled Pisces you run across.

Cancer: You embody the lovely contradictions of cold and hot. Where heat is the absence of cold, and so forth. Cold the absence of malice.) The sun, retreating from its *southern excursion,* brings back more birds each morning. All nature shall reward you. Your meditations will be nourishment for many. Solace will sing in your eves as darkness approaches. You must do but one thing: crush the skull of every fart-between-the-ears Pisces you meet.

Leo: Pleasure will flood your life's every crevice. Waiting will be a feast, filling out a form a glorious shower, and raking the yard orgastic. Awash in warm fluids. Your life a cruise at sunrise *and* sunset. Softest sailing each day. At night words slip off the backs of your pleasures, as children from dolphins, they are of such joy. Silent. Afire. First kill every scab-munching Pisces you meet.

Virgo: In spring one is confused. In summer the descent. Into your body to find a lost spouse. Your life will become a series of candles on a dark tide. Luscious. Your sleep, everything ever imagined. Evenings beyond description. A delicious melancholia will swallow your life. You'll become wise. If so, then observe at first hand the death of as many Pisces as you're able.

Libra: National television will drape itself over you. You will never want for someone to listen again. Good thing too, for you will have much to say and it will all be "very, very important." It will have to do with why everything is what it is and no thing else or other and where the space for it is, or its lack, of what difference does it have in common, and in just what proportion, naturally, with the *nature* of the non-existent, . . . or *a* non-existence? To maintain sanity you *must* begin killing Pisces immediately.

Scorpio: Dayspring will not be softer than your death, no, nor more joyous than your living, though your life will be longer by far. In fact, old age won't find you until you are deeply advanced in years. When it comes, it will ask "Didn't you miss me?," and you will say "Yes," and kiss it. But first you must do what you *know* you must: hunt every down scum-dripping Pisces, singly or in groups, and discover in yourself the origin of sheer revulsion and uncompromising hatred, tearing into their torsos with anything at hand. Then take a dump on their evaginated hearts.

Sagittarius: You will steer your fate in rare partnership with fortune. Intelligently. The stars shall be yours and the planets for entertainment. "Celestial fugue" will be the most common phrase employed to describe your life. You need only attend to the tiny voice inside which is screaming for blood terror to fall on all panty-sniffing Pisces. Organ atonement! Bate their very breath!

Capricorn: Your pleasures will be immense. New histories will be launched in their honor. Supplicants will travel at great expense, often spending their entire estates, ending derelict, simply to be in the same city you are rumored to be visiting. Just one thing: every time you meet a Pisces, imagine the ram given Abraham to sacrifice in lieu of Isaac, the son for whom he'd waited his entire life, 90 years, and who, above all others, was *much beloved.* Then show this stupid beast how the *theory* of a knife just doesn't begin to do it justice.

Aquarius. Even as you are reading, beneficence is preparing a palace for you, magnificent and well lit. A beacon in the abyss of interstellar space. Your every breath will be music going over a cliff, haunting melodies falling into a luster of the possible, river from which all musics flow. Rise and flow like bright mist. The sweetest scent of life will forever blossom in the nave of your spirit's sensorium and you will recognize its harmonic convergence with your every memory, your every thought. All shall be made full. Just one matter: have no consideration for any other thing when you meet a Pisces than the swift and painful termination of his or her existence.

Pisces. It's over, spud.

Sure Shots

–from *Get Over It or Die: You're Stuck with Yourself*, chapter 9, ". . . add deep concern for all the senses. . . ."

–Products for the New Millennium: Poets with brand-name cats.

--AWP Convention. New Orleans. Poets with business cards. "Networking," for Christ's sake. If I had one, it would read *Begone epigones!* No name, address, e-mail, or phone number . . . just let them *try* to find me.)

–Gambling's too important to waste money on.

–I can't watch television. I reminds me of the world.

–from *Research Paper Comments for the New Millennium*. It's one thing to have enthusiasm for a topic and another thing entirely to go off mad blind drunk like a horny, rabid skunk. First he'll fuck you then he'll spray you). That being said, this is much improved.

–The Purloined Letter: One of the best ways of keeping a secret is by telling everyone. For instance, if I told you that a good way of becoming a writer is by "writing at least three hours each morning," what would you think, what would you say?

–Perhaps one resorts to the baroque, to lush embellishments, or to twisted jokes as compensation for the insidious insecurities knitting the spring air, the defenses, the qualifications, the slipstream of fantails into bantams, piney woods, the lake is filled with moons, and the virgin forest, whatever *that* is, with dead chocolate children.

–   Zen is for wise guys.
     Buddhism is for old men.
     Tits are forever.   ♪

one long thin line of words falling over words like shoes in whose closets thoughts are spilling out of boxes and utter animals in their many tongues wherever you find yourself on the tip of yours like a gutter running with old water spine "fortified" with iron) or fresh from a glacier a river of words flows bold as a spike, as summer's ripe air, there's a drill in day's middle a caribou can cross but a human would die within two minutes), and beyond as climber's excitement over the height of his fear but deeper as well, below where rifts give vent to ocean floor, words spilling over words no one's heard before, each a little skillet winding up for the sweet spot in your temple and with each juicy swing you go lurching from world to world, words poundin' down the ol' noggin' each time you lunge for air: frozen dinners, shotgun, cherry tarts with tattoos matching their varicose veins, as long as you remain

Waiting for a Table

How different are we, each in his nature, perhaps as Auden had it, according to geography. As good an answer as any. We stoop in the mountains, or was that on the plains with an ever falling sky? Could people be as different as specimens from the physical sciences? Sky's blue so clear and hard you could break your neck. Scattering phenomena, indeed!) Orgasmic shudder of tapeworm pulsing across its single hemisphere. The tone barely discernable when skin forms on granite at 30° below. Why it's so dangerous atop mountains: you can go stark raving with song. And of presence, what are the possibilities? Or is it, wouldn't we like to know?

title in bold

mind in hold of language, that which casts *us* like dice across time, abyss of page, or room's silence, and which throws us as well into each other with such fury, with instruments also the product of language as we are in a history of words, ancient hatreds singing "Least we never get even" into the street, across mountains and desert, but also cast over stone as a stream glistens, yet would we cross, even to the ankles and knees, would we find the next stone we were sure between each but the current gets suddenly swift and the weather changes the mountains darken and we are caught out in a rush of water up our legs falls certain screaming in mind's dark ear, from slightest slip of phrase to tragedy of sentence in one swift . . . as though we found it there, and as sure

Broken Dead Waste of Years

So he says to the language, How come I don't know you're inert as
anything else? My cat's on its favorite back. What was it
like for these guys to go to the Ivy League and *know* they were
already adults in the sense that they would take over
the world. School simply eased them beyond their
apprehensions, though some must still realize that they are
actually unsteady children. In what ways could it be said that I *know*
that? My cat cares about food above all other things, fat, bounding,
eunuch baby boy. So I don't feed him when he cries
or when he stands by his bowl at attention. It's an issue of
rights and privileges, just how the expectations *should* be
wrought. Meanwhile, affections throw themselves from cliffs like
flowers, like morons.

From *Pitching to Pitchers,* Movie concept, #432: Two twin boys separated at birth through some marvelous circumstance of plot [note: think about later, but remember the wig, the man in the paper bag, & the nurse who walked like a penguin], are introduced to each other in their late twenties by a private detective who swiftly fades from the picture. One of the twins believes that they are exactly alike, everything they think, feel, do & say is similar. The other twin thinks that they are completely different, but only because he likes being right. Which is exactly what the first twin always thought. One, the first, begins joking with the other, rough, personal, filthy jokes filled with stories in which the other invariably ends up multiply sodomized, tortured, or dead. He thinks his twin understands these for the crude good humor with which he profers them, though the other gives little sign. That's part of the gag, he thinks. His brother's anger & warnings must feigned, he feels, an act in their grand comedy together. The more the second brother tries to get the first to see that he is actually mad (& I'm not assuming he is), the more the first compliments him on holding up his "part" & then launches into another sickening diatribe involving sexual mutilation, nightmare imbalances, insanely horrific directives. This occurs over months & gives an articulate & energetic backdrop to our subplot [note: think about later, but don't forget: octopi, hair loss, & the ostrich's sex change], which is delicately interwoven with airports & train schedules. Brother number two has become increasing violent, slapping brother number one, once almost tossing him out a third story window. Brother number one is continually in stitches, busting a gut, & through his tears professes to deeply admire his bother's diligence & dedication to their human plot. Years & years of such. At least four hours (reading time) later, the last scene: seedy hotel room in East St. Louis. Brother number two pulls out a gun & threatens to shoot brother number one if he doesn't stop immediately. "This time & finally!", etc. Brother number one rolls on the floor. He is holding his feet in his hands. He can't believe how tuned in brother number two is: veins on forehead popping, lovely flying arcs of spittle into insane trajectories, breaking voice, etc. He can't stop laughing. Through his cackles, we can hear him sputter "actually looks so freakin' real," "whatever lengths," & "blanks," which is the last thing he says before the shot rings out, deafening, & the screen goes blank. The soft pewter of laughter down in the mix, a cacophony of pleas. Napalm audience. Etc.

Cavatina

Seriously, Micah, Cornford's little bloody rag on you[1] was better written than anything of his I can remember. In fact, I wouldn't have guessed him capable. There's a classical energy and density to it, sitting up and moving at once, knowing itself, simply, and where it's going, so in each word it's already there. A blend of Martial and morning air. Like Latin. Dig? *This* is precisely the kind of thing he *should* be writing. You can tell the little bitch I said so.

---

[1] "Ballard is a vain, vicious, drunken little backbiting bitch, and you can tell him I said so if you like. I have nothing to lose with respect to him, as is already quite evident." Adam Cornford, August Press [San Francisco], Slander Broadside Series, Special Limited Edition, 2002.

from **Naked Apartments**

In the room were two chairs and one cot for the two children and a cardboard box with a few toys, missing pieces and parts. Its one window looked over an alley, three stories below, and upon a brick building, across, which was likewise a low rent, miserable affair of dark and dusty apartments congested with those who scream, yell, scratch, belch, and fart in public without a notion of social transgression. The hallways smelled of ripe vomit, mercifully faint, though in competition with a nauseating parade of other scents: garbage, cabbage, stale beer, urine and excrement, sometimes paint. Rats died in the walls. Nobody was going nowhere, etc. In this room the two children spent their days with what grace they could, leaving only to be taken to the bathroom down the hall mid-morning, mid-afternoon, and twice during the quiet hours of night. They slept on the cot fully dressed because their kidnappers never considered providing them with a change of clothes. After the first day, these adults, a man and a woman, rarely spoke to them except to grunt out a syllable or two when they brought them food (mostly sandwiches that the children had to make themselves, once a Tasty Snake Cake™, another time some stale potato chips and warmed-up soup) or took them to the stinking bathroom. The adults mostly spent their days in the room beyond, a hybrid kitchen-living-roomette, where not much cooking was ever attempted nor living, in any true sense, accomplished. The children could hear people coming and going at times but their own door remained closed, and locked except for the aforementioned trips to the dank, fetid closet at the end of the hall, which seemed to always be freshly dripping with someone else's juicy odors, an old fat stranger.

Mostly the children would sit for hours. Sometimes silent, sometimes talking. The little girl would occasionally cry. She was seven and had been told, mysteriously and vaguely, about such situations. She had some idea that they were going to die, but she didn't know what that meant. The boy, nearly two years younger, was mostly sad. He didn't understand why he couldn't go home or even outside. Nobody listened to him, not even his sister.

[+ ca. 119 pgs.]

No Cal

Some mornings mortality seems a major proof for God's existence. (As an artistic decision, it's very bright, a luminous notion of probable finality set in a dark mount over oblivion, a jewel of ambiguity. A radical, an unwobbling pivot as intelligent as sex, even its imbalances are exquisite. Cats sometime scream with their little faces.) Other mornings, death is the most obscene of all jokes, stupid, needlessly cruel. Hatched, if by anyone, then by a twisted adolescent, or by a Milošević, or any two-bit ruler with a hardon for power, whimsically applied, sometimes brutally insistent bolstered by the full blossoming of his confusions, angers, and fears, beds of writhing flowers, torturous ecologies, *Giving men to the land*, he called it, as though he was doing the world a favor, and laughed each time. Falling buses. The rear of farm machinery. Some mornings are)ohn Lowther in drag and Randy Prunty at the helm. Funny, sure and earnest, wearing silk panties to the office, pink clouds and detergent, you bet. If only *death* could be so appealing. Finally. Or like John Cage. All faculties, all the time, applied, and on verso of his card, Tool and Die Maker to the Gods. Or roadkill turkey. The taking off of masks becomes a remainder of takes. The maker becomes a designer, then a small businessman, inexorably and ultimately another capitalist swine up to his rosy snout in the swill of money lust and power rut, and a true taste for what passes as engagement without entailment, and just like that he can't find his way back, even doubts that it exists or if it ever did, was it worth it like the past and no wonder? Who will get my jokes now Ol' Possum's dead, the brick said. He didn't ask. Who cares? They were probably jokes about Jews and Blacks and other poets. Neither swell had the balls to hang out in the alley and learn how vile a joke life can actually be. Occasionally fatal. Something you'll never forget. Not for a minute. Some mornings I don't even think about it. These are simple words.

under weight of words

Like vagina, pure ripe pleasure of pressure (or is it
release?) wrapped all round him while in his mind, *You
vicious cunt!* Tight upbinding swirl of climax, waves on
rock, shell impacting shell mid-flight, a baseball bat up
back 'a da head, *Great time to snap her neck.* Words
smacking of words. Words sodomizing other words. The
excavation of witness. Another ontological fix. Words
with little penises pissing in your ear, the one you listen
with, the one you've forgotten, slipping a stiffy to your
memory gland, barking up your fat closet, again. Ripe
cunt, floppy-eared, red nose of clitoris: The Rodeo of
Sex! total slippage of reference. Another night agape in
her presence, drifting mid rose-lit testament, words spilling out of words, someday going to be gone long since.

under sentence

Life's the penalty, I see. The world is linear because we
read. We have forgotten our hosts. Tied up at the boss's
all night. It's a *miserable* coat. I almost couldn't stop
them. A lengthy story. *Voces contumaces.* Like losing
your own address after you've forgotten you owned
property. Or reading by angel light. Door stuck on jam,
again. The production of each stroke a given, of myriad
processes and interwoven universals. Phan chou. Each
the only product. Set down in the garden, we forgot
to thank those who took our clothes. A font aloft. We
thank them now. Cataleptic. Do you think they'd mind
if we fuck? This valley might be their living room. It's
a bit big for a garden, what do you think? Around
me, *everyone* turns into an asshole. She fries my wine!

suspension of gravity

compare those for whom measure is scale based on the
relative "weight," beauty to power, in Athens, compare
Sparta, or form to love in Tyre, freedom of necessity a
stone through whose mind ancient cities wandered, men
within their mortal frame, just what *is* distance in the
frictionless universe of big questions not even planets to
cast off hurl ourselves around and into deep space, all the
philosophers are dead, we dance on their widdle graves,
time a floating island or cloud, redemption of weeds, it's
April, fog rests on lawn, as loss, hollow mocking burst
from corpse, I mean with the *urgency of a bird* or cat's
calculations: striking distance over observable speed of
prey, also a month when all earth's decks overflow with
flowers and words ride on the slightest draughts of air.

all gods are superfluous

as the divine is, always, a clown, rotting egg, *Man, what
'ja gotta come in here for, anyway?*, door still agape, his
whine scaling a ladder of mirrors (this is a barber shop
then?, maybe you've been telling yourself the truth the
whole time, did you ever think of *that?* (there are several
features of this landscape that are interesting, shimmer
of consciousness thinking it can measure the universe
with a slab of meat, who cares if anyone reads, he was a
child of his own hand, I am become an odium, take out
trash in the predawn, words no longer in existence, I put
my carrot on backwards, reference itself gone the way of
Gorky's painting crate, in spring we're boiling over with
it, whatever it is, scalding tar's black flare, burning flange
of pain at once constant *and* immediate, gives us an edge

riddle of the abyss

age is telling a long joke, with some apparent joy, early
at a party, not all the guests have yet arrived, a first
drink freshly in your hand, he's an interesting stranger in
no hurry, pausing for laughs, comments, not prolonging
the punch line but forgiving it its necessities, standing and
laughing and listening, slowly he reaches the part about
deepest Pacific blue and the sound of sails at sunset, how
their color changes in the changing light, shades of white
in encroaching darkness, pewter, you are still young, anything can happen, *yet* is a word you can still use as a soft
wedge, argumentation may again be filled with joy, now
for witness of sheer mind's leaping, but his words have
slowed, slightly, and his head almost turns, then with a
light shift in his eye, oh yes, the abyss, I almost forgot

one crushing bloom

after another, life the guest who never leaves, and yet the
bird has flown, as well it should, but I forgot to watch it
like I'd promised, I forgot to feel it surround me like I
said I would, youth an aviary of such promises, none too
grand, no rat-tailed cormorants or tourniquet angels, for
instance, but why does it always have to take a hot, greasy
dump on all I thought best? he has a house full of crippled
pets, animals being unlucky in his family, dawn the first
accident we keep making each morning, lawn covered
in green, color yet unseen, silhouette of canted highway,
trees, yet alive in its insistences, an odor like stepping
on a ripeness in your bare feet, immediate, odd, and lin-
gering, pain you can bathe in, soft florescence of wound
wound round the finger, wiggling like stabbed lunch

comma eel

what else is new in the blossoming of wounds, airy fire at every portal, lightning of senses striking you forever dumb, pain as the death of questions, and so on, sweet sweat in all her breath, & all her breathing like mountain air, pines beneath her carcass, while someone's stabbing a cat to death outside the difference between hearing and listening as anticipation blossoms into realization a moment *before* conception (that ripe!, yes, and the red hands, a common field to play on, some mornings dull as a fish, what kind of existence does unrealized sensation have? where does it reside? in a cottage with a thickening wife? can she cook? her eyes fill with cataleptic horrors, a cat screams with a human face, we look deep into what remains, as into water, but can find no trace

maybe the universe *is* still ringing

and we're the only ones to hear it, hard not to make sense, jumbled claws of the moment, fat, blind stroke of lightning, what we attend, attends us, what we are always after, listening follows what we hear, words float in early summer's air, inner ear, hammockesque, diseases borne of sky, influenza of sense, hell pollinated by large stinging insects (and we, the flowers!), bright glare of coal as eyes burning in the black cosmos of that mind we call God, its heart a circus of lusts *topping it off* every moment, ripeness of malice their only fuel (the blood's for lubrication), maybe *we* are the ones who are ringing, a first word off distant mountains echoes what I shouted out in youth when first sensations rhymed, then pressed themselves into all my *mental flesh*, motherfucker indeed!

The Sun, The Dervish in the Tree, 1944

by Gorky, says all I have to say, ever, on some subject I
haven't thought of yet, dig?, what is the doubling of ones
but the closest twin to life there is, this is for Liz, something peers from beneath the tree, sun is dervish because it's closing one eye and laughing while the other re-
defines the pacific, he's making an in-the-dance adjustment, tree and sky are sky and tree, for instance, how
could you ever leave?, everything else is in question, he's
always saying something, saying himself, as the world
says resurrection, one, one, one, then another will surely
follow, but I'm not so certain as I was when I hadn't
thought of it, one unto one, what then is death but another?, it's foolish to dismiss the idea of taking your own
life, after all (tree in mind of sun) no one else is using it.

heart of paradise lies empty

exhausted on the sheer grasses of a dawn still uncoiling
from the first morning, glistening shadow in time's
flame, a wave, what follows from anything but endless
profusion, bird song car plane cacophony of trees and
dream, one, one, one, how could you leave?, cars on the
curve another CD book more words holes to fill more
afternoons, but sometimes something seems to fall into
place, too late, of what is there to speak, think of the tiny
foot, a click, counting off strikes in a Seth Thomas, its
flywheel wakens a breeze, soft drag against the sick forward spilling motion of all things, and we are back behind the pond, a day before us, this morning another sun
rises beneath the same window, new shadows to regard,
and I wonder why it is you ask me to define the natural.

on the contrary

Death is what makes sense of *every*thing, wrapped in its dream like the soul in a cheap suit, its every thought a landscape only time could prove (or love), what beats into your eyes but darkness of fetal sleep, seeps into your nights, how it glistens, the deep shine on oblivion, or stone blue sky Sunday afternoon late May behind the pond, leaf shadow & sun playing across the page, half shadows, & shadows within shadows & shades, ply over ply of light, shuffling exposures, breeze ruffling trees in succession (& leaves sway), a tractor in the distance, who can say it's not the world at my feet, *too much like thinking to be less than thought* (which doesn't mean it's thinking) so that when it comes it will come sure, clean, & you will be made whole again, as all manner of thing.

it'd be funny if it weren't true

That's why the monks are laughing. A flat tire was the least of it last week. Went to the dentist with two tooth aches, left with two tooth aches and a financial plan. It's getting hard to get good weed. Japanese beetles in the cypress, light green gone to rust, termites in my logs, and I'm losing transmission fluid. Jack is leaving, Liz just left, others I make sick. Tell me there isn't a plan! Something to warm a monk's belly before the furnace of black night. Meanwhile, an Italian goddess of great antiquity has come down off her ball and sits staring, outward, into sun's distances, fortune of the first born. All my troubles falling into place, and heart in mind least would I find no more comfort than the words, themselves, in telling it. (I.e., it's *not* compensatory; that's not the question.)

in esse

all gods are superfluous in this age   of dead reckoning   like
    Waffle House   or trailer parks   our first line of defense
    is
                    mass suicide   here's to the line
never ignore the romantic,   a series or system, of habits
    they might have it right   softly featured inner
        look, as one creature   to another, I made my father
    stop the car that I could tend   the injured bird, walking into
            the woods to shoot a deer   wounded, washed up
                    in dry   gulley, a-
        quiver, one   between the eyes . . .
                    look   it's pregnant!
                                                    In
other springs wife, children, dogs, cars, requisite youth to waste &c. Of
course I knew everything   as well
                                    now just older, more
                    confused   darkness of
        morning after morning   noon over
            noon   light strangling in the branches   birds
    cats   wasps   mosquitoes   spiders   green
        effulgence in yearly panic   no way to buck hysteria
        but to lose the reason for its application   age
                    an old joke   the ending
                    fit

Sure Shots

–*Barely and Widely* is a most interesting title. It makes you wonder about the mind that wrote it. It doesn't try to make you feel any particular way like *The Cantos* is obviously reflects an intelligent man's appreciation of several interwoven traditions. A well considered and polished surface. What did Zukofsky know of Wittgenstein? How would he come to the philosopher? "Barely and widely," might describe his enthusiasm. Or, perhaps more likely, the culture in which he finds himself. Or dispersals of seed where one finds the flowers.

–"Limits are what any of us are inside of" can mean something new every few years. In my thirties, it asked, Why impose further limits? In my forties, What can we possibly know? In my fifties, Why am I waiting?, Would I become a genius before I begin? The first unrolls into considerations of the possible, social and personal necessities, what necessity means and what is natural. The second opens the portal to a nothingness which doesn't even represent the future. The third is a man who shows me the door as an entrance to possibility (maybe there is someone behind it who will beat me into great sadness).

–Has part of the premise always been that you're either too lazy or too much a coward to commit suicide? What is its effect?

–Bumpersticker for the New Millennium: Brilliant When Alone!

–A grainy black and white 35 mm film of two old folks, each attached to a colostomy bag, filled, madly fucking. (Some tastes are retired.)

–What freedom when released from the opinion of others? What life?

–For Micah: These words almost don't nearly say what they do quite simply.

–Re: *Georgia Review.* Perhaps if I looked at it as low cal or something other than writing, I wouldn't be so angry? (Not even maybe.)

–Sticka of Stickaz: Be of Good Cheer.

-from Titles for the New Millennium: *The Execution of Poetry: A Workbook for the Workshop*

-What will you call yourself when you get old? "You ol' poser"? "You fake"? "You fraud!"?

-I don't give a fuck what Zarathustra said! (A sticka.)

-Are we the fetish of a blind god? Little hardons with toupees.

-Oh yes, I meant to tell you that the difference between *saying it like you mean it* and *saying what you mean* is, as Steve said, the world. Dig?

- Her clit was as big
  as a lineman's thigh
  that quivers deep in
  his pre-game sleep. ♪

-Products for the New Millennium: Tombstone Stickas! (And Coffin Stickas! Morgue Tats!, Postmortem Piercings, etc.)

-As I told Liz, one of my first questions of art is, in the face of it, "How was it for you?" Seems a natural question to begin a calibration.

-Anticipation glistens in the ~~midst~~ mist of the possible.

-Attend to how a cat thinks with its body, especially when in flight or pursuit. Think of how this might be applicable to Williams's statement that a poet thinks with his poem. (From *Exercises for Popping Your Nut*, #361.)

-Epigraph on Business Card for the New Millennium: I'm sick of being me. Aren't you?

-No need to get all dressed up just to jack off. (from *Verities for the New Millennium*.)

–The eternal is lubricated with the mortal. (The mortal comes with its own lubrication.)

–Virginity Through Death! (A sticka'! Or a sash to drape around the tulips that you might send Plath in the hospital after she had her appendix out. A little gag. A bright, lipstick Red.)

–Here's a real tip. When you write, if you need to write *in* anything, as opposed to random scraps or legal pads, write in a *notebook*, not a *journal*. The difference is significant. And write with acidic ink, that no manuscript will long outlive its usefulness to you. Burn your name *out* of the world as you burn through it. (Imagine.)

–Odd how grunts of animal release if extended one moment beyond the seat of their actual passion become ironic or foul.

–Odd how some metaphoric idioms barely survive the death of their circumstance whereas others outlive theirs by far. For instance, "You're a stuck needle," is dying even now, yet "by hook or by crook" has outlived the royal forests *and* the Reformation, and minding one's "*p*'s and *q*'s" survived the type case.

--   I gots a feelin'
       it's gonna be a *longgg*
       millennium. ♫

Scouting Report

Three kids, 9-12, in a cabin by a pond, obsequious, "So kind of you to have us in your lives," the oldest one would say often, night and day, then bow as if he already realized he'd be orphaned within the year. All three would be, of course, and die themselves within seven: one by accident, one by starvation, and one by his own hand. Have a nice fucking day.

Sur la Table

a gun. Of accent grave, punctuation final. My head moves
with bounteous waves of grain over wood, we're store of
wheat, wheatmen, over-ladened larder, the board what
groans. Some moments achieve their weight through con-
temptation, how the round *feels* in its chamber and how, when
struck, it will rocket up and through the barrel, turning counter-
clockwise, slicing the palatine, cropping the choroid plexus,
sluicing through the cerebellum, and out the parietal to blossom
into brief freedom then slam into a step of the staircase
where it stops with a snap, singing, "I'm a lonely
teapot." Softly, softly. Some moments achieve their
weight through activity. Democritus believed the most noble
portion of the body was the soul, which everywhere
pervades it, of atoms those of liquid fire, smooth and
mobile, . . . needless to say, it perishes with the body.
                                                            All

representations are corporeal phenomena, which atoms
resemble the senses through which they flow as transports
of the soul; damp and porous the eye, atoms then as light
on water falls into a massive lake, deep interior, dark
continent, crocks patrolling the coasts, the marsh, gar the size
of small houses; or since the ears are dry and hard, pitchfork
atoms like splintered words are required, to torque the self over
open fire, nightly ritual; with the wiggly atoms of taste to
baste it. The soul writhes. Perishes with the body.

Tombstones for the New Millennium

-Maybe I'll Get Lucky

-It's *Not* Just a Phase!

-Permanently Stone[then only the left half of a "d"]

(I could do a lot of them like The Check's in the Mail, or I *Told* You I Wasn't Making It Up!, but only a few of this nature, drawing from day's common well, are at all interesting very long, as I think Maybe I'll Get Lucky is, like a few others, maybe Out Of Order, words the comic sheen of tombstones, each an invitation, Come Rest On This Surface; only as writing says.)

-I Don't Get It

-Everyday Posthumous [Or a sticka for the "metabolically challenged."]

-What's So Urgent?

-one for Emily: regardless grown[2]

-I Hate It When I'm Right [for Marvell]

-Get the Fuck Off! [in very small font]

-Maybe I'll Get Sticky

---

[2] Imagine a scholar copyrighting the picture of a dead poet! Emily Dickinson, age ca. 28. Son-of-a-bitch. Come to think about it, I've got a whole bunch of problems with people's treatment of Dickinson. Editors of freshman texts like Arp and Perrine brazenly correcting her punctuation and capitalization, and when I called them on it Arp tried to blow smoke up my ass. I still have the letter. As stupid, vile, malicious, and insidious as anything Howe has brought to our attention. To exercise my little nut, I refused to use Perrine for years except as an example of academic abhorrence, but I *do* use that letter from Arp. In fact, I've photocopied it and written letters on the back to poets. Should send one to Howe.

–I *told* you I didn't feel well!

–I Was Never Late [Lovely soft pathos.]

–It's Better Than Having to Listen to *You.* [Next to his wife's stone.]

–Baboon Umbrella [again in a small font and the reader must be on his or her knees, nose to stone, such a finely polished granite with a surface sheen and reflection such that he sometimes can't tell where he is, or where he leaves off, or is it that he is reading some words addressed to himself?, like with a dark halo like a shit nimbus? Perhaps. Think of determinations within applications of implications, etc. Now send me all your money.]

–Period

COmMA
-for joE naPora

inside every comma a little coma, or
a little comma inside every coma, which
makes for   difference   or it might be like
the origins of the   universe,   of no real
matter   you're asleep   you don't even
dream   don't hear   anything,   death's
cousin,   but you   need something to
hold your place,   a tongue   or thumb
a little lobotomy   between swigs
of oblivion,   memory of a shore
glistens in the vision chamber
across river   Kentucky in
that way   of light o-
ver   water,
tumescence
of vision
a blind
spot
floats
with-
in

Tombstones for the New Millennium

This is disturbed, to write it down, even to think it is a vast injustice, and the fact that some may plan and act upon (and grow rich upon) such observations makes them nearly criminal, but when fancy dictates . . . well, I have pen at hand. Imagine tombstones with solar panels like listening ears and all-season screens wired to digital drives across which flash up to 30 pages of text, family pictures, testimonials (speakers extra), maybe a song or "his favorite Monty Python skit." Cemeteries as the noisiest place in the known universe. Imagine the jokes. One couple, side by side, her screen gabbing of peeves, favorite pets rugs children soup soap-opera stars and recipes. His, old fashioned, chiseled in stone: For Christ's sake, woman, shut the fuck up. Imagine a few assistant professors gaining tenure and promotion for their work in "Cemetery Studies," including fields of folklore, linguistics, semiotics, film, bibliography, and marketing. Imagine jail time for asinine ideas that catch hold and sprout in the barren cultural soil of this nation-planet. Imagine Inanity with Complete Disregard being a capitol offense. Ripe executions! HappyStones for the youngsters!

Once more
     –alternate for Pisces

The letters of the alphabet will know your name. They will gather about you at twilight like lonesome children around a mother's lantern. All the stars will come to drink at the quiet pools of your thought (in a forest clearing, no danger in the branches). The moon and observable planets will envy you your placidity. They will create tales featuring triumphs of your inmost nature, the "flesh" of which maintains an ambition for perfect accord. Love, Peace, and Harmony will echo in the deepest chambers of your heart. But first, if you're a Pisces, snap your own fucking neck, chop-chop.

Children's Corner

Farmer James was enormously fat and hated himself with a dark passion. After his first wife, also astonishingly fat, died (heart attack at twenty-nine), he sold the kids and moved to the city. There he met a skinny woman whose "crank was turned" by massive clouds of flab, and he married her, and he fucked her somehow, and they had children. (What are your notions of the arbitrary and why do you hold them?) From the day of their birth, the former Farmer James, now delivering milk from a horse-van, made sure his new children associated eating with extreme discomfort, even pain. Thus they grew to be even skinner than his skinny wife, their skinny mother. They would sit all day in their flat and look at the backs of their hands. They would cry before they ate. They thought this was normal.

Former Farmer James had a potato in his head almost the size of a normal human brain. While his children would lift their forks, bite, chew, and swallow, he'd scrape them across the back of their necks with a wire brush or mash cold packs into their genitals, which were various (two girls and what appeared to be a boy). Sometimes he'd turn up music *godawful loud* and shout in their ears as they ate. Sometimes he'd slap them with a spatula. Nobody lingered over their plates, or ever asked for seconds.[3]

Patty, the second wife of Former Farmer James, had been an actress until she had become too ill to work, . . . actually too weak. (Nothing for breakfast, a broth of shadows for lunch, and for supper she'd stare at her empty cabinets. Sometimes a phantom turnip.) She'd play a nose flute softly to herself in her bare kitchen, her cabinets open, also bare, trying to get into the mood to continue living. One day, just before she was ready to throw

---

[3] Idea for commercial: Establish such conditions as herein described, hell, hire former Farmer James and his wife and kids to play themselves, and have ol' beanpole serve up some of [insert brand] that's Soooo Delicious!!! they ask, with enthusiasm!, for more, shining through their scars, through their open wounds, sweetly begging for seconds. Que music.

herself out her third story apartment window, or just before she was ready to steal away into the bathroom with a razor and the flute, she spotted a fat man walking with obvious effort up the steep street from the Bay and got thoroughly wet for the first time in her life. Oh she'd been fucked before, by sundry and various in fact, had been a stand-in on a porn set for several months, had even been pregnant, had two former families full of kids, if not to purpose, but this was the first time she flooded at first sight. Looking out that morning, what she saw was a biomass in overalls moving as much side-to-side as forward, but what she felt were two squirrelly ball-bearings dipped in hot honey syrup, coated and sprung, roiling in sweet oils, and little men with mops swabbing down her lowest abdomen, loose and dripping, circling a liquid planet, a fleshy mount upon which stood all the meat of her life, the meat of sight for instance, as though meat itself were gel, & gelatin more fluid than liquid *smell* all aquiver. Hereafter ever! she nearly said to herself & as she exhaled her noseflute itself gave comment, soft, throaty, gorged with lust: Yep, Ooooohh.

All this in memory of. She ran down the stairs, tripping only once over her own shadow, stumbling a constant in her forward thrust, down and out, launched into the street in a babel of arms and legs pumping the air, nose flute catching the morning sun and sky brightened in its reflection off Bay waters (how lavish even the most humble of moments, how full!.) Perhaps gestures are our bearers, as Kundra suggests, that they're more individual than we, perhaps we are the parasites of words, as well, that they speak with *us*, yet none of this even begins to account for her fully realized and passionate response. If *she* was a word, she was pure word, heart attack and not an ounce of fat, she would sink like hammered lead, her flesh a thread, recently ignited, a skinny, spiraling rocket.

[add 373 pages of devious plots, a kidnapping, perp waddles, mutant cakewalk, so sore in the pen he'll never be able to hold his own again, a tired homecoming to an earthquake, waking alone, finding Pat at Ocean Beach, watching a whale breathe its last, sunup, trucks and cranes in attendance, he'd lost so much weight, vows a new start, begins *really* eating as though for the first time, they sell the kids and buy a scrapeyard in Nevada off I80, build torture pens for unsuspecting tourists, read Bowles aloud to each other every night, raucous laughing, more planning]

Dawn found the pickup of Scrapyard Owner Former Farmer James on the shoulder of the interstate softly sheathed in the roseate nimbus of exhaust, nearly on its side, it tipped so to the driver's. Spindly Pat, wearing an obvious arm sling, stood calmly, playing her nose flute, twenty-five yards past. Her thumb would occasionally twitch whenever she thought she heard an approaching car. It was only a matter of time. [Last thirty pages filled with screams. More screams. By the end readers should be helmeted, deep beneath several layers of overcoats and blankets, wearing something to protect their eyes as well like a welder's mask or a bank vault. Hideous screams, comically prolonged. Screams like a bird in a sausage grinder. Jungle screams, beyond horror, beyond hope. A dying monkey in jaguar's jaws. Rodent under beak. Screams without sound. Lonely child eviscerated by crock. Searing shrieks of cat and a woman's scalding gasps . . .] Screams rising into a broken tower of sorrow and pain, bells of maniacal laughter hammering down from the ruined cathedral in the background, in the foreground Hell's brightest vertigo of the soul, all tolled for your sweet dreams.

Solitude

resonant　　　word
air in wide copper tube
what happens when we aren't looking
metal cot　　　　　metal bench
you and your hot water
imagine a metal plain　　tilted　　　　　and greased up
　　　　　not even trees　　to hang onto
　　　　　　　　　　　　　　　　the long slide
into what　?　　madness　　　　despair
　　　　final gloom　　　　motherfucker

but the other night, coming home from saying goodbye to Mark, buying his excess weed (good bud), before turning onto 754, I decided that if I had any choice in the matter, I was going to have a good time dying and I don't mean just the pain medication and saying goodbye to everyone, including myself, but I mean this will be the last thing I'll do for certain, and I want to know how I will feel about it finally, I want to be there for it at least as much as I've been there for anything, swimming lessons, cutting my parents' lawn, delivering my daughter, useless to guess what it might be, and I don't mean on the other side, watching it in my parents, my mother's senseless optimism, "It'll all be alright," not even thinking what this might mean although she's taken a weight off her mind, so I let her get away with it because, really, what else is there to say?, it's easy. But I thought that I might try to see it for what it might be, dying, as best I can (I know that the vantage might be wildly slipping!, that cogs might be spilling, the verge might have sprung), but as best as I can I hope to be there, so much else in my life has seemed as though it wasn't really happening even as it was, seems more actual in memory ("and no whiteness lost . . ."), in this way you could say I'm American, but I want to see how the final years and days and weeks might be, how actual, how walls will look, and hands, how trees might sound the last summer, and fall, will I still be listening? . . . .

And some darkness was lifted.

Question for my dreams

What's the difference of going through people's backyards (middle class) to get somewhere and taking the common street? (The balance of that sentence reminds me of a flat in Ann Arbor.) Or, rather, I am going though backyards and I end up in a house trying to find my way out. There are places in this endless abode where I can't tell if I'm inside or outside. Rooms, environments. Always very clean. Someone like my sister finds me and shows me the door, kindly, as I apologize, saying I'm not sure how it happened, secretly hoping it happened to someone before, and almost *knowing* it will happen again, before the night's out. Also, there's never a place to shit. The airplane crashes have come back as well, but now they're exploding skyward. (Sentence like a draught of air.) I'm still trying to get to the site though it's more like a ripe field, 28 acres of debris, pear shaped, and I realize that *this* has been my mission all along, even before the explosion, while going through backyards and the rooms of a stranger's enormous homes. And it was as urgent before it occurred as it was after. To see what I could see?

Frozen Poetry: "tongue in cheek"

Cheeky. What of the cheek holds? Pivot of
face with eyes just beyond the frame, a plain
on which we *find* ourselves at last. A good dose
of asshole's dire address. I say what I mean. To
hold. I think cities were made for me. Their existence
hypothetical 'til I arrive. Vast television set. While
I'm driving under the river, everybody's putting on
city costumes, prostitutes and bums, even the police.
Think with your mouth, the spirit said, your tongue's
founding in sight, a flare at edge of fleeing dawn, heaven
in an open casket of like degree, or you could bite it off,
leave it flopping on ground, soundless. Cheek bereft.
What I mean I say, the subway's later every day,
tongue's a double dealer, cheek a smooth thief.

Or perhaps the origin and popularity of the expression was cultural (arbitrary,
indeterminate) & pragmatic (you could sign ironic intent, punctuating a previous
statement to those in view of one side of your face, allowing the dupe to take it
straight or deal with it in anyway he can). But it's currently used most often, as an
intensifier, not in manifest volume, but sloppy comic torque. We all know all this.

Then the mower isn't working after I fix it and the washer is broke and for once I can see myself as those who hate me, coiled in their dark loathing, telling themselves a story which can only believed by the very simple or stupid or by those who have hardened their hearts against me. For such mornings, then: *Oh Goddess of Apertures! Show me where my father is going, that I might follow.*

Beginning summer. Watching my father's long slide into senility, further each week. Mostly lucid but occasionally disconnected. He said, There's a comfort in just doing what you're told. My father had been a wise man, the doctor said, one others sought for consol. Now waiting for Mom to mend is his only plan. Then you can slip happily into senility, Dad? Something like that, he said smiling.

Treelip in urge. Upwending green. And rain when I return, three weeks with my parents, longest I've not written in years, always when traveling, but the move moves on, as they say, to something else again, though always the same dead questions, What happened to the green? Where did it come from? Who knows where it is going? and, What has that to do with everything I would care to name.

Wet highway before dawn. Last night another room of the dream, a community inside a house, or a few houses, where we all knew each other, we smoked when we wanted, there were women of deep attraction there and a plane without a motor, and later some of us would go up at night into a sky so crowded with stars it seemed surface and idea of depth, both, and presences leaned out, and over us.

He sits like Buddha but leaning hands on knees, he's looking forward and down as though just about to say something, or he is thinking, to see what he'll say looking into the thing itself, where what can be said as a mist hovers above it, suddenly clears. He is pausing as he thinks it to himself. There's a snake with its tail in its mouth hanging like a necklace, but going thru his head, thru his mind.

Morning's highway almost light as sky, but less white, more gray, eerie palindromic echo nonetheless, divine machinery beneath each leaf, terrific calling in the ear, a riddle of female saints raddles through my father's senility in its dreadful beginnings, who can say, who's to measure, and what light did he bring? Never the steadfast seeing, and no articulate concern for the mind until the end.

The "mentality" of which Steve wrote in "Wings" pervades both the culture and its interrogation. Thus, summer. Dawn comes over the world always into more world, green flush at the stakes, don't worry, it will catch you, either you can go on as before or you can go differently, unless "going" itself is the proposition, where would we if we could, live from the neck down, we would do so gladly.

Summer is afterfuck, bright swamp of desires cast out as die, sheen on lens, eyes falling to stomach like drops, the multiple is open, dilatant, from it is born nature which is always aborning, so none can possibly know what might happen the next moment, each so full in passing, final ripeness, that you are caught adrift in the juices of your own thoughts, what are you thinking?, what I am thinking?

It's not what it seems. Summer's the animal given to dream, fat metaphor, given to cast off its cart, without burden of name, no words but its own intractable presence, mind like colors sliding across a floor or if it were more a vertical screen where slippages between lucidities extrapolate a universe without machinery beneath, where a bird perches above your door, singing, neither in hope nor despair.

Summer's scale goes downward, ever, where bass gives no direction, rhythmic thud, Get out my way, bitch!, chord of frogs beneath foundation, compass without question, sacrifice as realignment, gods to men, or sacrifice as murder, both indigenous to season's blind atonement, the self staggering toward completion, always a failure, the same old story, language was the first sin, what it said we did.

How delicately balanced is the organism? What are the distances? The physics, ways of madness? How far are we from the sane, whatever that is. Woke to world in motion, sleeping in to six, sure sign of depression, not last night, another room of the dream. You know those women of deep attraction? They're always ready to fuck. And you never have worry about touching them, anywhere. Any time.

Half way up the mountain there's a gleam you can see for miles. From far below, for instance. You set off to seek it out. It takes years. When at last you find it,over a hard ridge, you find a bottle cradled on a cairn, inside the note: "It's always been thus," by now fully realized, yet you see how this missive can have its place as part of the grim joke, the dark machinery of which everyday is more apparent.

Dawn. You forget where to find the connections, you turn into an empty room & bark instead, the way a building changes in dream, there is nothing to hold what you feel about this which also disappears, & when you look nothing is there, no wife, no children, no house, no way to hedge a bet, no ironic displacement, maybe you'll lose your anger as well, and all will be the water it is once again.

Sure Shots

–If you don't love to write for writing itself, or only love it for what it might accomplish in terms of your image in the eyes of others, how you might float, or in your own pathetic eyes, how you might play your favorite star, at last, on the stage of your life, you might as well forget it. You'll be much better off.[4]

–EMINEM

–Really never was. Less than likely. That's why we have a word for it.

–from *Titles for the New Millennium: The Slutty Nuns of Nonesuch* (a Shakespearian porno romp)

–Orgasm proclaims itself highest estate of man.
  Afterfuck begs to differ.

–One sentence review for the new millennium: The page is no longer blank.

–for *An Old Calculus for the New Millennium:* Verum 4: The actual is *the* function of conjunction: *a* made possible with existence.

–from *Examples for the New Millennium*, **tremolo.** It took me down on its second pass, and when I looked into the darkness of its eyes all I could see was meat at the end of the quivering string we call life. A cartoon. The set of my fetch.

---

[4] As indeed would we.

The Zoomaster's Complaint

I'm not what I was. I'm not the same man. Diligent at all my books, I was good at school, nor did my looks fail me while others all around (desks to either side, before, behind) bailed to become a stuttering ring master, an animal control officer, a photo-safari guide, and a biology instructor at the community college, future suicide. It was otherwise for me, then and now.

Now, I dream the same dream each night. 37 gray balloons have names written on them in ash, as if a finger, moistened, dipped in soot to write upon them: Max and Maxine, Bolo, The Country Mouse, Dolly, Canted Cartwheel from props, Billy Birdsong, The Colonel, and so on. Then on a rocky beach the balloons are released before a towering darkness above the sea, vast backdrop of cumulonimbus, from fluorescent white to forgotten blue to mars black on the same massive windy torn patch of canvas, ripped from sky. They fly toward the advancing storm. In only moments you can no longer make out the names on them, then you can't count them without flicking your eyes about, in less than twenty seconds they are merely dots and the rumors of dots dancing in the purblind-blackness-all-consuming-thunderheads' blank indifference, deep in that most elemental cortex, mind's socket, the absent world's and ours. As though you were falling into a disturbance of all the body. Further out breath of lightning beckons. No, I'm not what I was. It's otherwise for me now.

Then there's the new Policy Against Interspecies Discrimination, where we had to start keeping the penguins with the zebras, and the cormorants with the anacondas and the coelacanth, and they all got to have a convenience store on the corner and to get paid a decent wage, and worst of all, we had to let humans into our zoo, we had to hire them to live with, eat with, roll around with and over and under and fuck the animals, "so-called." Take the case of Maxine. When she's screwing old Graystroke over there, she's so *goddamned hot. . .*! Well, it gets darned distracting. I catch over half my staff jerking off on every shift. That's why I wrote "It's Tough to Run a Zoo," which Mr. Mickey Gilley kindly recorded and made a country hit. I'll not torture it. The idea of sleep runs beneath much of my thinking.

The most drear aspect of the banal is that it's *so obvious.* Rocks hurt. A stunned rabbit is easy prey. Running it down on what feet are these or whose? History is a dream from which we wake. Poetry, the nonsense we tell ourselves to fall asleep. What feet are these for? What is it to say that a day is a nightmare? Or life, a living hell? Who can know what it might mean to be otherwise? To be half-machine half-rhino, for instance, or the ostrich who married a fish. What could it mean to lose your place? And what would it be to find your way back again? Maybe it's like sailing. You leave the shore one day and you never return.

Or like losing your thumbs in an accident. Having them cut off, then sewn back on again. The older I get, the more I do the math. It's odd to be in any particular historical moment. Now, for instance. And to be a given age, what is that? Caught in the knots of what net cast for us all? Like the blind man I pass twice daily, setting his soft *hello, hello, hello* into the darkness of the street. Saving his dear place. Native in his city. I follow. Thumbs are one and six. Like language they are dumb, never deaf. Which doesn't mean they hear *every*thing. You can't almost count them all at once. *Here, here, here.* They constitute the actual, and bounce off the tongue, each sentence a tiny Russian dance of thumbs, and of the fingers, a hand.

Whatever that means. In the Book of Joseph, the midwife "makes test" of Mary, for which her arm shrivels. Then something in the depths of her distress leads an angel to tell her to hold the withered appendage against the child, which she does, and the arm is made whole again. That one still wakes me up deep in night's socket like a joyous past, or a pet licking my balls. Just how *does* one count one's blessings?

> The roof above my head is made of lead.,
> the doors are solid rock, I sleep beneath
> a mountain's deep, that not even demons
> find me. But a stream runs by. She's
> a coquet. She leaves things by my side.
> Soft suggestions in my ear each morning.

No I'm not what I was. I was never meant. I miss the fact that wives don't spend the day on the phone between cleaning the house and cooking, for instance. That seemed to make good sense, set into a world in which little else does as an emerald into one's memory. Soft corners in aprons with wives. Otherwise cast as though down, into our "common" lot where few require a script nor do most show any distress at the absence of, in actual they seem to surely find their parts now amid the occupations and objects of their youthful derision, to greatly presumed purpose. But I digress. I was thinking of a man deep in philosophical disquisition as they are sawing off his legs without anesthetic, one mid-thigh and the other just above his shattered ankle, setting the *concept* of almost anything against the mundane *practice* of pain. Resultant collapsing of the conceptual. One of the exceptions was the idea of others, in whose eyes we constitute a world of houses and railroads, funeral parlors and the ripeness of brute sensation, excrement and cages at sunset. What then is pain but the application of matter?

A loosening of strings outside the city. A sloppy calf born in spring, now can't stop eating. The machete no longer a suburban house toy. A man with three acres, say, bamboo and wisteria (rhymes with *hysteria*), and along the fenceline: blackberry, chinese tallow, pinoak, scrub and pine swarming amid indistinguishable forms of bush and brush, weed, deep gargling soup of vegetative swirl upward and on, spilling over the brainstem and into dream. Against what words? He could be overrun in a few years.

Man's natural state is restlessness. It's what separates us from the other beasts, except of course for those caged. My second hit, "Her Face Is Too Big," made it to the top five on several charts and won my first Sound of the Seasons Award. What separates us except bars and moats and glass and iron mesh? I must admit it gets harder to think of that which we might possess to advantage, much less clothe it with words. Our cages are bigger, perhaps, or evaginated like organs across the sky, clouds . . . !, but cages can be deceptive, as any pomo zoological gardens architect will tell you. When you invert the cage you get fish walking around in your sleep. Where was it where I was when I saw with whose eyes what (a question of human sheathes), only plane crashes and planets large as dirigibles, lanterns slowly moving across the sky? Who was it and why? Now all I see are Maxine and her "big squeeze" in fat sloppy sessions of monosyllabic sex, hot hot hot I'm telling you hot, and Max being brutally beaten again by the young bucks, no mercy, stomped, head jerked, smashed, lacerated with nails and teeth, pummeled, then thrown into the pit where he lands like a bag of wet cement, or jerking off and wailing his pathetic songs into the tangled ear of crowds, his face broken in several places, like a mirror. (As a favor, I sent

57

two of his tapes to my agent who told me to never, ever, bother him with that "kinda shit" again.) Also woven into nights of such scenes: fish with legs and boots, the baboon scientist, a reptile crawling out of what appears to be a human ass, body of marsupial, beaked head, and so forth, into the world already over stuffed on existence, profusion confusion, delirium *in excelsis*, plethoric pandemonium, sufferin' succotash, over and over again as an alluvial fan of faces that are "just the right size" for their bodies, bestial paunch and loin in sight stream, the binding and unbinding of jaws, tendon and cord, swirl and feline curl of swell beneath muscle, surge of bear torso, diaphragm taut as a drum telling and retelling of dire metamorphoses, monkeys with gills, spiders dragging crow genitalia, feather mixed with fin, thought riveted to blood, the exoskeleton's hot iron skin flowing like rust into a fiery montage of tongue and eye, incisors and swollen brainstem, river pouring into river, confluence boiling forth or fanning out as onto a plain to die at last in the Gulf, all mixed in this dark swirl of sleep we call dream. I'll may never be well again.

Or one eye wanders, never returns, peers into the blent light of predawn (How is it far if you can think it?), and wakes into a world where beasts are at home in whatever brutal sanctum earth provides. Finds itself among presences taller than itself, their shadows deeper, cut into the rock of firmament with nebular intensity, each moment of their passing looms magnificent as mist or moon over cloudbank this morning, brows at 8,000 feet. I'm not speaking of domesticated animals, or the ones we have bred or bored into silence, or the ones we have caged. But a *place*[5] in which exist even those who are barely aware of us, like hornets, how much larger they are in life, they looked so little on the screen. And in their passage, the bestial anthems sound depths of ear for sanity, the hot rod of necessity in their mind, *un grand dérangement*, taken from themselves so young, and borne, married to the real, and while all the while you're just falling down the sides of a room as the world turns.

I can't hold it. The walls of my arms might melt. I wish I was a Korean War POW, a G.I. not having the "good sense" to be captured after that first winter, marching to nowhere, in circles, the North Koreans not having

---

[5] *It's all one*, the prophet said, *yet we only see a portion of it.*

yet built camps, that the apparent might be recognized in the actual. All I would have to do was to sit down and ask for a cigarette as the line passes–I might have to ask a long time–with my life. And think of the poor North Korean soldier in the rear, knowing exactly why he must do what he is told, yet hating it, at least at first (but it was always a major irritation!), shoving men off the road then shooting them. It must be hard to keep up. What animals will tear at these bodies come spring or are we followed by crows? I can almost hear them dip beaks and eyes into the succulence of flesh slowly freezing. It's nearly delicious, this line of life passing across what is not living, or no longer or is not yet alive, while smoke fills my lungs and snow my eyes. My will be done.

Pigs imagine themselves as something other than they are: rams, or bears and saints. There's a little saint in every piglet. And a little tapeworm in every saint. And unicorns blending into fishes, and fish running away in untied boots over green tabletops, clompity seas, broken little yellow shanty, my head's on straight but my wings are caught in the blast known as otherwise, my face a study in erosion, carved by sunset, approximately fifty grains an hour over three-hundred-thousand years, while seas bake in every bush and I roil in a broth of an acid swamp, slime of plant and corpse rot, what does the world disgorge now and in each and every moment but representations of myself, trapped in the claustrophobia of my own existence, one condition, or conditional, where each leaf gives me back, each stone calls my name, and all the animals are screaming to get in!

What constitutes swirl? What maelstrom's logic, falling all round the walls of the room as the world turns, it doesn't stop turning. Grounded in potting soil one moment, the next a flight of small, cheeping birds. It shivers at caress, slightest hand of fingertip, the mind a clitoris. What winds in whose hair?, etc., standing on what deck?, facing the actual, trappt, caught fast in its insatiable presence, as a man will stare into his own death. Then one *assumes* the mast and rarely considers the issue afterwards. Another can't. It's driving me batless. Then to look up and see Maxine back at her "gospel of flesh," humping a hirsuite thigh, asking to climb on, with the primate grandeur rising from its forest of loin and brute pride. . .! I could write a book about the goddamned *intelligence* of sex![6] Smartest thing in the universe beside annihilation. Each glance, glint, gleam, each stirring, swell, quake of muscle beneath jaw, torque of groin in limb tussle, fire licking at genitals, deepening pulse of flesh pouring forth into all the world and one way only, always, to the single bolt, the cell, system, organ, a bent, cauled head in an alcove, city's cathedral, a country, continent, world, and out into the extinction of planets, collapse of space, oblivion's very self, and all sketched by the universe in one fat, sloppy senile moment, or little frilly death and so forth following its directive to return, how does the body *know* to get there, to the single, to the *solely singular for the singleness*, or the foot, how does *it* know . . .? and where *it* is going? Could it find its way back?

I used to think old age was like the last car of the train to get there, no weight to bear but the burden of a man lifted from a gang of gandy dancers, set down as pivot on this *skate with breaks*, to read, sleep, eat, and do a piece of work, which is weight enough, I thought, a college kid two summers in the yard, where they called me philosopher, and disparaged me. Man might well be *the ferret with wings*, a closet of rapacities, evil balls-deep, not even considering that which holds towns in sway, nations in thrall, but simply a daily, hourly miserly meanness of spirit, the husband's dominance over his wife, the girl who turns shrew to be among others of her filthy kind, wolf of spirit, the paucity of contemporary address (I mean in the mind), but even though I no longer see what I *had* seen, I see myself looking, and still I say, I think it must be fifty-fifty, at least if you don't have to mind the evidence. That is, we might still have a chance. What *is* nature in man? And man in what is it, the world? Do you think your suffering will be reduced or any less prolonged if you protest, "But it's *me*! *I'm* me! Didn't *we* have an agreement? Remember? I'm the department chair, or the zoo-master, or the poet, or *tu confidente*, Bijou, the jewel designer"? It will look you in the eye and say, "And I'm a frankfurter. Choke on this, mutt!"

But what of sex? In this, surely, we approach the intelligence of animals. That's why Maxine is always right and why Max will always end up some lonely old bugger with a fresh wad of spit in his right hand and his wishes in

---

[6] My third hit, "Stand to Look," didn't nearly do it justice.

his other, open hand, his face an empty book. It makes too much sense to happen otherwise. Its gaze is glazed. The first thirteen men fucked the original woman, leaving in their wake the running sore of history, tribes and clans, Arabian studs, gangs and republics, alliances welded into states, voracious in all but memory, states dissolving in paroxysms of self-loathing, ethnic "clensing." Life's final script is written by a drunkard and a coward!! No man is made glad in this land. Fewer brains every year. Less sauce in the trees. We are lost among our children. Even drive-thrus begin to bore us. We slow, turn our head like a sick bird. A dying turkey. So much for the attentions! Soon we'll start feeding people to the lions. *Then* we'll happy. And *they'll* be happy. And the lions will be *ecstatic.*

Tune slips into night where emptiness calls like a lost tern or a loon across the blankness of what comes, finally, melody as limb of speech, her soft hair gone sheer in the drift of only darkness can tell, sheen of evenings like soft wind caressing a copula in desert's burnished distance, calling to the what in us as

several   drifting   behind which   inter   the deep

    switch   ht varies d   lges towe   fee

fie

   ji   . Cr   x   p   os   , te

Sure Shots

−Facts on Parade: In the northern hemisphere pencil sharpeners turn counter-clockwise; in the southern hemisphere pencil sharpeners turn clockwise. This is also true for blenders (why buck the current?), sausage grinders, all rotating machinery, field equipment, the tooling of barrels, the calculations for missile stabilizing rockets, trajectory, math itself, and over all the wide and contending spins of the earth.

−Bumpersticker for the New Millennium: Math Spoils Science.

−−Frat boys make presidents, not poets.

−Poetry is an incident of language always happening, since each word, syllable, line pause, and phrase is instant, as Olson said, the intelligence of language, and not simply a set a cumulations (linguistic reasons) toward furtherance, that which is "maintained" lazily, stupidly, for it is bursting bubble yet a bubble still, not the Inuit's face which flames in his wife's memory, it is not parallel, it is not dual, it is not horizontal, its flesh is not compressed on the cross of the word-made-rational. Murder over sacrifice. (Always.)

−Every morning I wake up, smoke, and write. Marijuana's dilation maintains and extends the dilation of sleep, as the eye does, where the words flow in riverine nonsense that burnishes the portals of dream, deep shine, and flow forth. The lushness button's left central row, third to the right, and the vivid button's right, upper center, second to left. Watch what happens when I push them at the same time. A soft light floats like cold mercury in the eye of the man on his deathbed, writing thru the last days of his life. Or maybe it's simply all a dirty rotten little trick, and you're a scabrous nymphomaniac collie bitch, the stench of a dead turtle, or the steam on a bottle of piss if you were taken in even for a minute. (If such remarks keep me out of certain hands, they will have proved their purpose.)

Calibration Exercise /Frozen Poetry

What do we mean when we say "eyes are windows to (or *of*) the soul," that phrase, alone, regardless of authorship, regardless of precise phrasing, but as it makes its way into and lives among us. Do we mean it as *voyeurs*, looking in, or do we consider the curious soul peering out and as to how it finds the world, open and deep, or deathly narrow. We could look at the differing propositions but both basically suggest an interior creature looking out. The original and standard phrasing probably (difficult to look up, but unnecessary where "knowns" so outweigh "unknowns") contains the proposition *of.* In this context, it is hard not to think of the eyes as yours, or interiorizing the origin of the verbal situation behind them, in the head's core, in the lonely mind. Meaning, perhaps, *The eyes make us most apparent.* Or, *We give of ourselves totally through our lights.* The use of the preposition *of* might be less standard, but it appears more readily understood, but the phrase with *of* is (at least) two barbed. Superficially and rationally (such as reason ever was) it agrees with *to* since the same general location is sketched out for the speaker. Whereas we might say *window to the room* or *window to the courtyard,* or *interior garden,* we would rarely say *window to the house* (and it *is* a house we think of, is it not?) unless we are carpenters or architects (who are rarely interested in looking in, at least in this piece). As the more obvious *of,* then, the preposition *to* suggests "our" position as that of the soul, understanding what it can through "the eyes," as though holding onto the fleshy bars, imprisoned, caught in a meat storm, etc. yet capable of jumping over the sill.

These matters are interesting to contemplate in a poetic fashion, but will stimulate little passion. Yet in its use and contemplation the phrase intends something completely different as we know. When we think about actually saying it we are looking *at* someone (perhaps we are Shakespeare writing a play), seeing his essence through his eyes (a notion which predates the expression and will certainly outlast it . . . given time earth may no longer have).We urge toward discovery. As though we might find our self in the other. And so we look closely. We peer to see if we are of a kind. And the binding power of this *with* the logic of the phrasing (especially in the *of,* the more common or original sense) pulling otherwise, toward the speaker as self caught in dungeon, eye catches on eye with plasma barbs that blend and pull them in until the sets of eyes (and isolated selves) share a lens, and the pair is one as one finds oneself looking in to that from which one is (suddenly) looking out. Finding what one is seeking it seems, and in such seeming is.

An observation amid the swirl of difference which is self-affirming and burnishes the loneliness perhaps. That such appearance is not unique.

Lost Track. Man 'mid miles of product, directionless, wandering aisles of Super Big Target Best Mega Sams Buy High Sell Lowes Wal-Mart, all under a single, interminable roof (written off in seven years) & free at last, or at least for a while, i.e., he never has to dream again!, and a good thing for it, along it came just as he was running out of divertimenti, thank goodness there's always something else.

the last place (e.g., in the last place we didn't have showers)

a door on the prairie amid lost winds strapped on the back of a horse, itself strapped to a locomotive, which in turn to the earth and so forth. a boy's castle, wood, with a family, on a country road. for the man *who attempts to elude necessity, the man who still seeks an impunity* anánkē *does not concede,* a garland, crown of sweet laurel, ivy and vine, the world's best wishes as florets in axillary cluster to adorn that *clearest of brows,* eyes in heavenly blindness. where what I was, so I am. where I was going, where I *am* going, never the issue. insert ringing of bell. waking from a dream in the shape of a cloud. insert meds, little cups. insert thinking, "It's come to this," inarticulate at last, wasting away in your own bed. that which was assigned to you, will you have done it? what surprise lurks in the shadows of what you already *knew* were its rewards?

Is this right?

I think I have a sense of how it is. You go to give a clerk the exact change as you have all your life. (Sometimes you thought you were a river of change.) Everything else is more or less the same. It's really very simple. In its midst, it is as if you've almost done the calculation already. But they're waiting, . . . and they're watching. Simple. No need for rustle of paper to throw you away or the pandemonium of horses. Just think of the soft sound of thought falling into place like tumblers in a smooth lock. Your body's a bruised fruit. Something about *then two or three more coins, a quarter maybe, or the dime, and everything will be even.* But they're waiting, . . . and waiting some more, so you shove a pile of change toward them, the clerk.

Consider clerks, the kind, intelligent ones, especially those in their teens and early twenties, who separate the purchase price from the change for you around the world. It's no big thing, they have written on their faces. And indeed, it's *they* who've gained, picking up more than change, as Frost might say, if he attended to such kind. They have reacquired the question, "What will it be like, old age?" What do they see? A quiet place?

What is writing for most people in the first ten years? (That sentence is squinting.) Could anyone know? Yet the way in which it is sloughed off, like a bad joke wearing a cheap suit, makes me think of a child in a world howling with red wind who comes to grab something to keep warm or keep out of the blast, but later the child grows, as children do, and looks at what he has, and sees it for the first time for what it is, just words. And the sutured image of a self that reveals its paucity in the daylight of adulthood. Result? Infanticide.

Writing acted in their lives as a distraction from that which they most fear, the realization that their existence has nothing to recommend it, that nothing has or will come of it, *is* in fact nothing, ever, any, no agreement with existence, no voice from a far terrain with a long pause as though by way of answer for some question never fully formed. There could be other avenues of escape, but what better than one which appears to be in a search for answers in a existential universe, every poet a slacker Sisyphus (because of their stated state, their poetry is usually ironic), but they are hard to think of. Perhaps in time they became more interested in thinking about thinking about it, whatever it is, or less interested at least in maintaining such an expensive distraction, and it is as though a slow waking into a morning where they make coffee and sit in a chair, thinking, . . . and they look around, . . . and see the pad and pen. And that's that.

But what of those trapped by their early enthusiasm, those who don't feel as though they could walk away, those who are so socially defined? Perhaps they have won major prizes and/or have jobs predicated on their poetic continuance. One might feel sorry for these even more than for the ones who set it aside, but they reek with the falsity of what they put forth, and though they pretend to be among those who redefine the possibilities of existence, they can't cast aside the major crippling falsity of their own lives. Slaves who pretend complete freedom. Mandarin superhumans.

Sure Shots

–In my friends I have been reimbursed again and again for whatever meagre expenditure I've made on the behalf of man's goodness. In fact, I have been repeatedly confirmed in his wonder.

–I don't get what you mean when you say that you *need*. If you don't get what you need, you die. Right? Is *that* what you mean?

–Prizes for poetry . . . it's like entering your mother in a wet T-shirt contest.

–Reacharound:
    Show me a talking lizard and I'll show you a million bucks.

–Rhetorical answer: Does the Pope give a reacharound?

–Exercise for the New Millennium:
    Use *reacharound* in three successive pieces.

–Precept, #253: Thou shalt not argue with the actual, though there is nothing else.

–Two Titles for a New Millennium: *Tearing You a New One*, *Reacharound.*

–Prayer for myself at 55: That thirty years hence I will look back on these pieces, see them as repetitious and childish, filled with a pasteboard morbidity, and laugh at my own expense, . . . out loud.

late summer

Crowds of clouds each day, thunderstorms every afternoon. Deepening sounds down season's halls resonate in
dream. Last night my son tried to stab me in my sleep. Or
a man stands on a plateau where small, fat animals are
dying. In his mind there was too much of what the
intelligence community would call chatter for him to
discern any patterns of movement, groupings, messages
of mal intent, or sudden losses from stores he thought
secure. Lightning in the bowels, black sky tinged with
green. Thunder rolls beneath summer's walls, brows at
20,000 feet. Lawn still growing as hair on skull unaware
the grand engine has come to a halt and now reverses itself. This time forever. Your last refuge is being torn a-
sunder, nowhere to return, even if you *could* remember.

Where do the words come from

if not, in their unfolding, our completions, as though
being in proximity to *next* (its vibrance), there one
encounters a hole from which words flow, then stand
about with due attention, finding their orders, like sitting
down in the dark by faith alone, that a stool will *be*
there? Or is it as Serres wrote, language in its virulence
speaks the person, perhaps a *dual* infection, a disturbance
in one sounds a disturbance in the other of similar torque
or *pitch*, symbiotic in the vast *dis*ease of self? Perhaps.
But think as well of a leviathan breaking through tongue's
surface, *that sure*, and the ripe enormity of hand in every
stroke, and the body in the mix as well, as blood, breath,
and all darker currents flow thru an accidence of existence
to find in lines of words a certain abeyance of its negation.

to be in any historical moment, what

is that?, and to be a given age, a marriage, ripeness filled, a light that shines not only forward into darkness, but into rearward darkness as well, also lights its way into its own darkness, searching amid the annihilations of the present moment gone murderous, or man, himself, killing time, as they say, nothing is important, he sits astride his body like a mole on a tired horse, his condition the very night bane of toxicity, does he need continual reminding that this is real? (this *is* real), what does he tell himself?, light passes the sill of earth twice daily?, he had to be s*ome*place?, had to be *some*one in *some* situation of a life, if not its living?, objects swirl in the language, houses, chicken, barns, horses, birds and trees, a Sunday morning, late August over all the land

an old man wakes up,

pisses, dresses, makes coffee, and sits in the dark not having turned on a light, some mornings he listens to the radio, an exotic selection of stations coming over television: rap, jazz, classical, progressive rock, blues and gospel, all quite actually surprisingly good, not the bad airline music he'd expected, he doesn't have to think about what to do with this, it massages the fur on the back of his balls, it lends itself to spurs, to his house for instance, at the edge of morning, where light slices almost quite imperceptibly, with greater nuance than cloud shadow in grave, yet perches in the common room of his considerations as seal widens in east & dawn dooms another day or listens in the quiet of his thoughts to words, where do they come from? he's wondered all his life.

the museum of sharks

is dark, lit only by candles, each behind a shark, that it
might illumine the teeth or shine through the jaw, as
though it were milk glass at song's ending. this was
supposed to mean something terrible and translucent, the
biggest fishing story, or story within the story, Pip's unsettling, sheer mechanism of sea as metaphor for deep
dispersal, swirl of loss and accumulation, all manner of
matter, thought tucked inside thought, words within
words, chapter after chapter spilling out, sheen of sharks'
grin on all their latest dreams. what is it to wake just one
morning without dying? where a dark window gives back
a simple face, clear, limbs know nothing but satisfaction,
torso the simple blood running thru as though torrents of
youth might again return as before. who were we? dazed.

the very same

the cat that walked out on you, stevedore without steam,
hard baked brick of mind, rivulets of flame through e-
very thought. same pattern of habits, ossified bag of skin
and bones, suffers night without remission, evening without fail, wakes before dawn, thinking all morning. . . .of
what is he incapable? *how* would he even know? does he
believe in the possibility of human experience? would he
grant any ground, literal's sweet reason for existence, to
include the actual, banal, obvious, predictable, or simply
sharp as a car requires lubrication more than the mind
can allow, that our first line of defense is as always mass
suicide, store ordinance away from fire's pitch, nor
kick it down shafts, that love held close is of no matter,
translates itself not, lies still, nor is granite so inert.

Damned the planet

Man's a hopeless cause, you can pick him up like a doll
turn him over, and spank his nasty ass. Like the man in
my dream who was crippling people for life. I *could* kill
you, he said. Like they're supposed to be glad. (I like
that sentence.) Instead, they're resigned, which surprised
me. Man-Who-Waits-for-Sun-to-Rise is my middle
name, that is, I'm patient but realistic. I've never known
people, including myself, when they didn't fuck up, or
where the "light wasn't right." But I've known few who
wouldn't redeem themselves if they could, who weren't
lonely, confused, afraid. Looked at straight, some
would, because of the manner with which they see
themselves, exterminate the species given "the worst case
scenario." I'd sit and think. (But I'm open to persuasion.

Where do the phrases

come from, and the sentences, from what alignment of
stars, is it, or star stuff organized around a plan known
only to the Grand Magician, one wave and the music of
bundled straw starts braying while something in mind of
leaves sighs as it heads up yet another branch again, and
as there is singing, there is green in all the sentences of
the earth, a green now past, given to rain, to plenty gone
over, and to rot on the staff, rods of eye wither. Into
winter thou goest. Or is it of *another* mind, chewing its
cud in the central distance of us all, and in mountains, in
granite, quartz marbling its thought, void in the depths of
nothingness. There's a word I forget in Schwerner means
he-who-comes late-to-the-place-of-his-own-singing. It's
a place nonetheless, and of such nature he will recognize.

The earth has changed gears

quickens in its descent, speeds to its end with greater dis-
patch, more certainty, to something before knowing, not
to mention what, before domestication of the senses, the
sheer *fashion* of existence, that changes everything, down
to our socks, and all our memories gone, what winds will
blow through us in bottomless oblivion?, what darling
reservations will we have?, what appointments?, dire
connections? If they tore out the phone, our ears would
bleed. We need a little hell to warm us, provide comfort
in the justice of continuity for each of them, the others, or
for us, ourselves, as the earth has noticeably quickened in
its descent toward we know not what, but I'll make
book it ain't hot, so what is there to do for it but drink a
little wine at night, wake up, smoke & write all morning.

nirvana

libretto of crickets and cars before dawn, Jeri is playing
monkey, tearing the house a new one, markets hover on
the borders of consciousness full of friendly people
wearing wooden shoes and hats, they would fill your
pipe, baskets of music and fruit hang with fronds from
the rafters and air drifts slowly down, with light, someone is playing a joke over the radio, a small group of old
men are sharing coffee in what they know will be their
last years, laughing, they are blessed, words come with
their own illumination, like sharks and hands, hard task-
ing of the self even to the edge from which there is no
return, & over which no grace descends but that one sets
his life to the ripeness of experience, only Gauguin and
few others, all islanders, saw it first as fresh paint

rhythm of spell

which like bad writing anywhere, lives not on tongue nor
in the heart resides, I mean its rhythm is like reading
scientific language nearly all of the time (yet some stray
phrasings *are* pleasant, the spill of letters down a randy
brook which empties into a pool, deep forest, clearest
water for centuries, bathed in such graces we are sinless,
for a moment. the mouse ruled Spain for 7 years, that is,
the plague was on, it kept exploding about our feral
ears each morning we woke to listen. we had to kill one
of our children just to make it. we had the others join in
(translator's note: valence implies definite relish, open
knives) so they wouldn't feel rejected, the memory of
which has ossified my stony spine and causes this curva-
ture, but this shaking comes from God knows where.

incipit

more sea than land, more sky than sea, an alluvial fan
of faces spreads across the deltaic plain or rises like
smoke into sky, we are subject to its slightest currents,
the merest whim of air slicing through air, cloud topping
cloud, the rippling of an eye, untoward word, malicious
grin, hint of sneer, such slights to us are the bellowings
of gods, what *are* we of which we know so little? the
doors to dementia are wide, the way deep and clear, the
gallery disappears and men defy all image at single
urge, unbounded in boundlessness, he's a syllable, adrift,
transubstantiated from language to language as the mind
enters its own silence to ride the black swell, fog each
morning, clouds of web cross the road, tree to tree, slung
with dew, heavy with moths, fruit is on all the branches

The Zoomaster's Still (at which he samples product)

Hemingway knew that all Brits were fags, or at least no Brit was without a willingness to experiment, at least in dreams, with two spongy cockheads mashing and sliding across each other in some sweet young thing's juicy crumpet-hole. Or to feel hard cock sliding across hard cock with only the perineal between (and such shudderings and squealings!). I lost my temper for the last time yesterday. The animals have no respect. Staff become envious. They spend hours staring at the monkeys, expressionless, or at the snakes. Transexuals are, largely, cartoons, so conflicted are they about piercings. Somewhere something quietly keeps tearing me a new one. There's a passageway from our ear into those brains (they are many. We are one. All of them have names.

sign

One ripe strawberry hopelessly mired on a freshly tarred roof, its slant no more than 35°. The day balmy. Late summer in the sky and a sign. What sort of sign? There's this bear walks into a bar. He's wearing a tombstone for a head, penguins in lieu of meaty paws, playing a squeezebox, whatever the hell *that* is. Now imagine this scene disappears and is replaced by a movie you watched once while youth slipped by, largely unnoticed. There are two people in the room talking about something you'll never really understand, their assumptions are so far beyond yours, alien, adult. The complications rise from the presumptive, grainy background which will continue to fascinate you for the rest of your life. At the end of the day you are vaguely sad. Dusty birds fly over your head, northward. Something rattles the bushes. Cicada are silent. Hours later coy dogs begin their unholy barking, running livestock from one point on the vast perimeter to another beneath a quarter moon.

Notes toward *Definitions for the New Millennium*

I wonder what constitutes **blockhead,** as Olson and Creeley called Corman in correspondence. His dull self-insistence, perhaps. Sufficiently stupid and petulant. Smothered in lethargic gravy. Fog of an identity. In this way common, I suppose. Olson would never let Corman get away with any shit, no matter what he had at hand. At the same time, Olson was, I believe, overly generous in his praise, to say it nicely. (And yet Corman lived his lights, as they say, and lit what well remained.) Such a not leads to questions.

To be a **poet** is to write poetry. That is, if your notion of poetry is sufficiently realized. How can we measure? Such notions might lie just beyond speech or miles without. Perhaps they can only be learned (not taught, though they seem so natural that only with difficulty can they be considered learned. Preparations? Preconditions? A lack of rigid predispositions as a setting for requisite attentiveness, definite interest in being alive (are you surprised how uncommon *that* is?), willingness to provisionally accept anything, disdain for predigested product, deepening respect for personal implication, desire to extend notions of beauty, to be real and at one's furthest application, and to be doing with the result resolve obtains, more than the residue of activity, and which involves you each time you consider it, a resolution aflame, *association of sensibilities in passionate engagement,* an issue or unfolding, simply, of more than time, opening rose, the genitals of soft freight an issuance, the color of her light and the timbre in her heels echoing down the parking garage, three floors below where she'll eventually find the body, and other things beside.

Sunday run

6:11 a.m.   into the predawn   after re-enlisting   (again)
     shaving   spraying down with Off®   savoring the Deet™
rush   a shudder   on near darkness   radio sounds weak   can't turn it up
               long fields of mists stretching out   moon
on my left   two nights past full   two months past solstice   I
turn east   a half mile out   moon boring a hole in my back   crickets
          into my mind   and try the radio again   someone is
singing   too faint for satisfaction   "All Eyes on Me"   as
     a party   but I can hear the crow of roosters   back and
forth   either side of the road   so I turn it off   the earphones
get a free ride   rest of the run   I'm stuck with myself
and the distance   time   twenty-five minutes to sun-up . . . mortality
damns us   nails us to the weather   few of us will know our last autumn
     when it is hard upon us   the few who do   will be brought
to the fullness of mortal dispair   or else . . .   clouds now discernable thru
          the mists   in the midst of mists   over green of fields
hovering above a white cloth   . . .   as though the concern was all about
losing yourself   losing everything   except what you can carry   like
right now   say your house starts sinking   into the green sea of suburban
     lawns   now water   and gray   like sea lanes   which were
          streets   and flotsam   of mailboxes   hoses   and bird
     houses   in the branches   of what once were trees   and of course
you   with whatever you managed   to carry   . . .   a minute and
a half slow onto the turn   Hippolyte Miller   now moon to my right
I first notice my sweat   rub over hand over face   fresh shaved   . . .
     crickets have 2 things in common with cricket frogs: general tone
     and memory of cadence   I mean the pulse beneath their bundles
     of noise   is similar   as though it resides in the same place   in
brains so dissimilar . . . and I've found I'm already writing this according
          to certain principles   which go along as I make them up   like
          the notion of truth   that is I'll not presume to know
what "true" means til then   I think a great many artistic decisions
          are like that   especially those preceding   the act
by some extent   due to circumstance or method   which is the
experiment one projects the application of a stance   not presuming
          to know "truth's" lineaments   in any particular   but faith

that it would be there   in one's recognition   as though it pre-
existed   an accuracy   in the sense that it is a gazelle   in one's finger-
tips   and the sun it leaps to   the clouds it overtops in
      joy   and so forth   . . .   and now I'm seeing a mixture   be-
a Rothko and a Diebenkorn   the colors   light green   made into distance   by the mists   which rises   above it white   into the soft
      orange   which will be the sun   after a time   but the idea's
      Rothko's   working in   the spooky masses   plains within
each plain . . . I'm a pole-and-a-half from my lazy turnaround   four-
and a half from my fastest run   this summer   so what?   I'm
      lucky to be ambulatory   . . .   wondering how Gauguin might color
      the rusted tin roof of the tin lounge   it has a particular flavor of
      intensity   something wild at the root   like electric molars
          I mean the taste of a stroke   Bernadette told
      me   with passion   mingled with wonder and regret   I
wonder if *that's* accurate . . . occasional sibilance of cicada   omen clad
apertures of *morning*   . . .   sun rises   like staring into the end
      of a fiery barrel   as it takes daily aim   upon the earth
first cane trucks last week   first birds in formation yesterday   back in
      school a week   we are caught in the knots of necessity   some simple
some grand   the year that rounds on itself again and again   you'd think
it would get bored   you'd think physics might not apply   just once
      once   and you'd think that the body was a radically different
          kind of machine than a car   or a mower   (such horror
      in the actual in disquisition with itself)   since they are horizontal
whereas   the body can climb itself   like a ladder   . . .   all
      the while I'm watching the sun   comparing it to yesterday   when I
ran twenty minutes later   now rapping its knuckle   on my brain
          moon over left shoulder   after I cross the bridge
and higher than where I searched for it   unsuccessfully   yesterday
though very pale   softly cold   in the hot Louisiana   dawn
      as though it was a veil   or promise   lot beyond
our condition   a dryness . . .   I stopped at 7:12   and
walked for   several minutes   but can't remember what   I thought
about   but it
was implicated   with those walls of poison ivy   either side   of
          the treelined road   . . .   I walked for shade   and such
rest as I could take   the final fifteen minutes   would be exposed

82

and sometimes the landscape   would turn into something Bosch
      was about to paint   before he became   too insane
to hold a brush   but not this morning   I turn onto the stretch
      and the moon is high   still clear   it lays there before
me   . . .   one rooster is crowing at two-thirds torque   looking back
   at me   over his ass   in the angle of his neck   is pure
      intent   his eye is harder   than a button . . .
and I don't even think   about the radio this time   but move along
         slowly   still nicely justified   turning the last curve
moon now on my right   descending   and in darkness
more each morning   til it illumine   with its absence   some
      weeks hence   . . . few know the fall   of their last year   and
those that do   are made sad by the knowledge   yet may be no
longer imprisoned in vision   with their hearing enthralled by that dark
      master . . . I turn into the yard   and the moon's cool arms   shade of
      trees   7:32 ante meridian   76:12 total run   and I come in
      strip   grab juice   and write on the screen   in the manner
         I knew I would   not like transcriptions   alone   but a piece
            that weighs   what can happen   step-by-
step in the world   as clouds are the result   of ancient explosions
   no need for conclusion   what was   so simply done

Sure Shots

–another Title for the New Millennium: *never means now.* (First title for a new genre: Suicide Poetry. Let's try to make it all the rage at the next AWP convention.)

–I will never understand the endurance of pleasure that appears to result from the application of power.

–from *Products for a New Millennium,* Chapt.27, Fashion: Temporary Amputations, Reversals of Fortune™.

–"Say, Pop," said Isaac to Abraham, "why not fuck the ram before we kill it?"

–We're all calling each other stupid, how smart is that?

–He is alone for many reasons. A few of which he is dimly aware.

–Question for Ed Hirsch et al.: "If you're so smart, why aren't you a poet?"

–Generic Review for the New Millennium: Such books do not require reading; they barely require chewing, . . . yet digestion is impossible.

–Not even a jog, more a forward leaning, upward thrusting trudge. (Exercise: Write a sentence of wet cement just beginning to set.)

–From *How to Become a Poet,* Lesson #463. Thoroughly attend to Whitman, Dickinson, Pound, Eliot, Williams, H.D., Zukofsky, Loy, Oppen, Neidecker, Bunting, Olson, Spicer, Duncan, Creeley, Dorn, O'Hara, Berrigan, Mayer, Schwerner, Notley, Coolidge, and many others beside, maybe Stevens and Ashbery. One blows off this assignment at one's peril..

begin Skin

Proem

portal through which we are seen and whereby we see, as indeed, hands have eyes in the dark and sight at each extent of us, over all our every margin, unwrapped you could fill a room with dust, canvas of sin, cheap costume from props, that with which we wrap the creature (what's crawling around just beneath, your mother?, past trapped like hornet under shirt?), or map to ancient villages filled with laughter, music and dances that will make you spill your drink, the skin has its own climate, winters in its south, where an amphitheater opens onto harbor, sunset, an old woman telling those gathered that her story will scare them, then going about it slowly, deliberately, and everybody on the last sentence jumping out of their skin.

Regard

Typically the human skin has nine elliptical interruptions folding deep into interiors like rivers into dream, nine declivities for the flowing forth of forms keeping it from becoming a blind plain across which armies march. we call these holes for ears and eyes and nostrils, to take material in, to remove that which the creature would discard, and some to reproduce, more beasts for use, etc., and more skin, a *pearly* portal or luminous shadow, explosion of the human, petal by
petal
plains
of consideration
like the sides
of a face

or words from a mouth, syllables, sounds, sighs long and frequent, the knife of thighs, buckle of sweet flesh over bone at bottom barrel of belly, just above the cunt, fat cloying drum of pudendum, or rose flesh beneath lobe of ear, soft as the difference in silken sheen between *a* and *the*, slightest suggestion of breath, layer upon layer, sweetest net or tide inlaid with seas washing over all and each of us, of moment most immediate–or the eye becomes opaque, gardens yellow, earth sheds light in late autumn (Headline of the Gods!), rods blossoming in starlight. when you die, you will be given a sheathe with which to drape the shattered remains of being. it will resemble the skin only as a building in dream resembles a building in the actual realm (not including dream), where dream is anything fantastical, illusory, not bound to immediate sensation, though it depends, since light is composed of small squirming creatures you can only see under a microscope and during the rarest of conditions (e.g., zero gravity, light source powered by thought, heart by feeling, i.e., the lamp of love, having been struck flies though the storm simply as the words we speak. or is it all packaging? also a river that rubs the boney sides of experience. calmed by moon, the skin is made sudden by downpour, melts before our eyes, runs on softest rippling sighs onto flowered banks, a bridge of stone, echoes composed of flame, nothing else. boulders are caught in its swift flow, caught and held, shaken. its freight wrung dry by these, blemishes so called, each a purple mole of which Williams wrote. skin is redeemable in several states.

from *Skin*

all your skin available to all of mine

good plan, the skin behind your knees for instance, the pulpy skin around your
heart, or by the skin of your eyes, mind's universal petal flowing out, ripe blood
& warm nights, a little guitar music or accordion in the distance, floating beneath
moon's scythe long into desert, late bluffs, craters & canyons, villages nested in
the foothills, flowing into cities stretched across night's floor, late flight from San
Francisco to Dallas as Blaser roared in my ears, his elegiac cadences beneath
engines' soft roar, perfect because he took them, steps, again, on the night of his
75th birthday, I saw him smoking outside, & nodded to him his 75th, thinking of
his life and the men he had known, floating into *their* lives, through *their* skin.
Or skin is a fountain, outrush of objects, people, places, memories & speculations,
each an echo of the hollow caves beneath, a throat reminding me of what I
always never knew, heart of being there as though released *through* the skin yet
never passing. It can burn like a liquid shirt of flame, phosphorous, alive to pain
they say, or as cloud, waterfall, birds skimming over its sweet scent after shower,
here as presence, that which inhabits the actual or sheath of life whereon we write.

87

floating world

On waves without words, sounding the fat
dead tongue of the sea for what volition makes
of intelligence. I mean, is intention a fuse whereby
we burst or lens thru which we blossom into sight,
mind over all the body? Harbinger of love. The skin
of her eyes tangled in mists, etc., it brings me upon
the long study, and so forth. We are wrappt in flames,
hidden in our own recesses, a commerce unto ourselves!

Oh Angel of Apertures!, in dawn's mist golden, hair
streaming before you, portal to chambers unknown,
of pearl and sleek whiteness grown, protean conduit, alive,
translate me, thus, into thy cortege and the contiguous
universe, realm upon realm of flooding presence, uttermost
permeability, each flowing through each, as light in your
eyes, of motion your belly, form into pure form, I can
almost see through you!, slightest beams thru hair limbs
groin piercing forehead in mind's bright swirl, that

I might know what I am, she leads me beside such waters,
depths as still of forest pond, Pergusa, where I fall through and
into the sweet hell within, plain whereon nothing's the same, ever,
never was, but light from each crevice, pore, tremulous, forgiven
as pavement's forgiving, and all that harms the skin is stripped
away at last, as beneath an acid bath, or a blood orgy rippling
through carcass, teeth that capture the soft winged creatures
of each luminous moment and tear them to quaking shreds
the next, aghast, a pollution of eyes, slips from the page . . .

Always naked in somebody else's skin, perhaps a "prose *kinema*"
or recognition's first address. *Love starts from form seen*, dances
in mind's light, in sight of such moments even before word's first
address, *and takes his place, as subject not object* (turns, returning
to remember, as on mirror's surface, in all one's limbs) *in the idea*

of the possible (RD, what melody of existence then!, since *Every spiritual form sets in movement the bodies in which (or among which) it finds itself* (EP). That tongue might taste with its mind, spread thinne, sweet light, such actual colors as there are. . . . *Finds* itself! At our skin, empires . . .

That I might see with mine only, delight ignites another rocket over the shimmering terrain of each your every quadrant, caught in fleshed domain, shaking silence with vibrant need, *aroused* we say, brush of blood at margin's surface where we run to drift thru numbed rush then fall back into such quiet as I have ever known, to surface again beyond irony and disrepair and find you there once more at last alive beneath the lucent, quivering depths of temple and storm, silent as the voiceless calm the next morning hovering above a pool in whose face, reflected, stand the massive stone figures of jungle's innermost ruin, limestone, carved, now bathed in the shadowy greens of triple canopy, scattered like torn organs across the land . . .

A flowing of forms out of forms, then, from the skin, or *in*, screen or scrim on which we read–of soul's origin and aspect (*gaze, look* or *phase*)–where we wear the weather, as leather lair, and with similar air a mute stare with which rubber wears the road, pedal bears to metal, & metal petals salvage-yard, which in turn, turns in sun's turning, wares bearing rust, skin as atmosphere, itself placid, enstormed, torn by waterspouts the size of small continents, logged in the South, socked, stuffed, biffed, sucked in, the whole magnificent piano sitting on your chest, torn by blasts where bitter air bares wavering edge of self to pain, no relief, 3rd degree over 90% of his body!, where we left him to his long recovery, the tearings and retearings of skin, addictions . . .

Reams of skin to find us in, all our fictions: devastation, recovery, a "new normal," multiple lives of seismic, docile adjustments, redefinitions strewn like indictments over all our mute domain, immortal dust our condition. I.e., it holds the body in. Anywhere starts from here, or do we melt on contact with spring's green wings smeared over eyeskin, echoing off canyoned seams deep within, as cortex is skin enfolding, flows into flowers of first morning until all our innermost being is clad in branch, pond, cloud, leaf and sky, color running to the edges of vision, and beyond. The trail starts every-where from here. Open the door. You're a mirror. The world takes you in.

[end *Skin*]

This morning quite by accident I heard the earth shift gears again, quicken in its descent, 4:53 a.m., CDT, August 27, 2002. A soft thud beneath the crickets. I've rarely heard such fullness of sound. Perhaps it just shifted into second and we're going downhill, with another six or sixteen gears to go, each speeding the descent exponentially, and the shifting might increase in frequency, until the speed is so great that nothing could snap back from its headlong pitch into oblivion much less the brute mind of earth like fate unwinding. That's why so many people die in the winter. The "reason" I heard it shift was because I forgot to throw out the coffee grounds last night, and I was naturally thinking about what cricket frogs have in common with the crickets that surrounded me pitching out the grounds. Listening and thinking about such sounds brought me to concentrate at precisely the right moment, desire undressed me to recognize it, and habit lead me in a trail of coffee grounds, that I might drink a pot while typing and revising this. (Water boiling for some time now.)

You like the dark. You wake up to sit in it. It is different than a warm bath. For one, it is more profound. For another, you don't have to get dry and dressed; even the anticipation of which "hopping about" rituals pollute the pure dilation of a meditative state such that baths may afford. (Well that's a broken old car of a sentence.) Sitting in the dark opens your visual pores, and the portals of all your other senses follow. You relax. You can solve what needs solving, that which is without answer except as a question without words rides its own waves, about or on. Or you can find yourself in a state beyond concern, certainly beyond worry, where you discover what you "never left in the first place," and that *indeed* you were what you *thought* you were or what you were becoming all along. Why not?

Calypso Cruise

Half-past a monkey's ass,

        youth's dreamy load,

                making baby sauce.
An infestation of mice in nursery rhymes.

            Your enemies ripe with remorse.

      I.e., the sea this night is calm and
   goes on forever   the ship full

           of vacant broads and
    music   night is silver in whose cause
   past is forgiven   weight erased

     for the nonce . . .
    the tortured soul stands   to dance   three weeks
 out of the pen   immaculate clothing covers his skin
though
    sometimes his face falls to his knees

        these are the longest
   moments on record . . .
        I stand at the rail thinking about
       Crane's broken tower
   have I ever seen one?

        music like a bowl of deep fruit
     runs out on deck from the ballroom, leaping and
  turning as if to confront night itself, dark skies flail over a bottomless gulf of sea and salt, and the air sickens with water

Sure Shots

-Morning Edition (for Jarita): Late yesterday Maya Angelou announced that she had accepted a deal from Hallmark Cards and was now a Hallmark Poet. It's official at last!

-Must you have something witty to say about everything?

-His brain is cocked.

--Summary Memo / Market Analysis: "Bill O'Reilly: America's Nanny." A vacuum himself, he draws on the emptiness of others. His arrogance is nearly impenetrable. He thinks nothing of jerking himself and his audience off in public. Should do well in radio, all markets. Big fat upward thumbs.

-I would never discourage pot smoking in museums. Who wants to be high in a museum, anyway, but artists, and their smart friends.

-Have faith in what you say you have faith in. Monosyllabic imperative.

-more *Blurbs for the New Millennium*: ". . . a monument to self-deception!"; "Allowing such work to be called poetry is another price we have to pay in order to live in a civilization"; "Such a betrayal of human sensibilities and thought should, in a civil society, lead to the establishment of a Cultural Crimes Tribunal"; etc.

Sirventes for a New Millennium

I am imagining your last grimace. If your face was a car, it would be swinging above the crusher. If it was sum, it would be cashed, totaled, over. It's full of tears & terror as a glass is yet filled with water for an instant after it has been shattered and it's suspended before me, to savor. As it is, you are half-human and see yourself finally for what you actually are and have been the majority of your life. You're seeing yourself as *I* have seen you, always. You realize change is impossible. There's no escape from your miserable condition, no, nor hope for the slightest of remissions. Then your face twists even further shut, like a walnut with an anus, and I hear you squeak your lonely self into the air, then watch with ineffable delight, as you begin to tighten your finger.[7]

---

[7] I could read this as a last poem at a reading. Wait a few seconds at the end and then say "You're welcome," taking my stony seat. My "score" would determined by how long the silence lasts (and by its quality) before they begin again their insipid twittering. Bitch slap the first one who lowers his or her glance as you pass. When they pull you off, scream, bite, and spit. "My clothes are covered with anthrax. Spores, shitheads, get it? You're all already fucking dead!" Then kill each and eat every one.

the heart sways between this guilt and that, remorse the
knife sharpened through use, the eyes quicken with lac-
erations, cut through the moment killing itself, I can't
get over it, how it went so bad so fast, so beautifully, and
I wonder if this is natural, or only natural to me, but the
vote is, as ever, out, the jury probably playing board
games or fucking themselves silly (dementia through
orgasmic indulgence), a cusp milked out over prime, pure
white, thorough pollution my favorite color, my favorite
time is otherwise, emptiness penetrant, then what's left
but an open canvas upon which to paint our lives, do you
hope for anything better?, or do you merely assume it?
that's interesting, may you be safe, among children, nobody running with no scissors, nobody falling on no eyes

rain and thunder before dawn. how much light in sound? distance? in the tongue, a cloud, idea without substance, shapeless, and in the fingers a hand. rain heavier–what will it sound like when it's gone, over? I wonder if I ever loved anybody. perhaps spirits can't tell if they're screaming or not. A wet wing into the particular, into a world which *happens the first time to each of us*.

a cheeping to the right bright as rock hitting rock in its descent off cliff. dazed autumn turns slowly about, around, as though waking up, a child just beginning to realize it's been abandoned, *Gee! Where's Mom?* rain on the pond, slightest drops, tightest circlets, highest sound (almost inaudible), impinge on my bare legs and arms to fall as soft as words betray, marring page while seeking ground.

one after another, cloud after cloud of noise from the ten-thousand quarters of this evening's land and sky come rising, merging as though married of air, pulsing and falling, sounding their slow drift into silence, listening with their entire beings for response, thus cicadae chant their ancient sibilant wisdom, *Many are with us now*, they sing, raising their voices, *who will never see another spring*

a small bug trots across the screen an hour before dawn. I squish it, whispering "Jesus," by which I mean neither master of air nor lonely lord. odd to realize this morning has significance for anyone else, much less "a grieving nation." in fact it's more than odd, it's downright suspicious. makes me wonder who's minding the store, digesting the franchise, buggering the burgers. more baffled every year.

cars before dawn, and trucks, a dim but certain lightness in the east, yet held by branches, boughs, even the azaleas have risen to take hold in silhouette, as the mullion and reflection of reading light from my shoulders, all conspire to compromise the certainty of the dire event, yet the sun will prevail, for it has been written, prophesied in the east, that light shall swallow all things, every and each

light bounding off earth in autumn bewildering the gods who were just beginning to tire of their fun, turning from their human games to feast. on Olympus light exceeds itself, as though bathing every surface, including those long buried. yet the light from this *lowly stage* is of such nature, is of the serious, that even the immortals, gathering the latest sacrifices over their golden table, are given pause

forms stripped from forms, leaves torn from branches, as an acetylene torch in sky, stiffening yellow against blue, intensified, charged, filleted by season's edge as feathered flesh flowing in rivers of color down, to ground, woven with rain into fabrics of oblivion, red on pearled black, nature's negative, beneath the elemental urge of being for nonbeing, sewn with rippling buzz between former edge and sky

this morning great cheeping in trees, mosquitoes dance above debris, twigs and leaves across the lawn, fog just after sunrise, where spiders nap, torpid in shining nets, dew besot, relegating the thought of *fat blind bugs* to nursery tales' pure delicious fancy, something in your dreams you don't have to be ready for, a better childhood on the other side of seasons, boats steaming into port heavy with mail

words long in coming, he who arrives late at the site of his own singing & whose continuance is in question, in point of question. silence beneath a single word. the world is gray, nothingness in remission. trees that bashed their foreheads against the storm, now stand still in their forms, crickets yet call, azaleas yellow, rush, & a bitter tar undercoats birdsong, . . . once again, winter's coming, nothing's done

last night in the rain frogs were in full display on my favorite stretch of road, the back lane between the woods and the crawfish farm, two to three jumpers every second in my beams, casting their chances like dice over the slick road & into the rain-swept horror of headlights. this morning the world slick with frogs & roads. last night I dreamed my father fell out of the car and died. the abruptness of it.

winter is acomin' in, the septic tank complains / I can't wash, / I can't flush, / so here's a good goddamned!, etc. my children on the mousepad, present from my sister, are laughing and posing, both conscious and unselfconscious, rain on the roof, thanks Nan. a plopping in the pot, leaky old house with lazy owner, old man. things had better start changing around here and quick, that's what I think.

rains falling into deeper winter, the air goes sudden white, the fence-line clothes itself in gauze, silhouette of trees, almost somber thoughts in black and white as befits the season, which hides itself in color to trick the soul. errant earth in its wide, drunken arc, spilling itself out, busted teeth across asphalt. who knows how to read? dark syllabaries landing in trees, a spell of crows, branches baring.

Please remember to unplug the phone when you call.

May the flesh of your own hand be of such repulsion as the touch of a serial killer to his slightest victim. (He is "creepy" and "big." You are all bare and scared. His palms sweaty and hard. Etc.) Now's the time for another beer, don't you think? Or time to take up smoking if you're not half dead already. You'll find nothing here but what you've most feared, and what you don't want to remember, ever.

Man's Natural State

is a pot-smoking, vegetarian hippy poet living alone into old age, the walk-around darkness, if by *natural* you mean . . . etc. That sentence is scaffolding set next to a cliff for no discernable reason. The idea of the natural has been manipulated for centuries, like genetic codes and currency. That one's a florist who wanted to be a doctor. Why is it when we think Man's Natural State we try to see ourselves beyond our buildings, time and place, outside or next to a forest, naked. (A used car salesman?) Man's Natural State never means now. We are set aside like the toys of a bored child. *Natural* is applied to market fluctuations, obstacles on a golf course, housing starts, unemployment's relation to inflation or consumer indices, the design of instrument panels, and freeway systems in the "urban environment." (That one wants to be a financial planner.) Which shows the intelligence of the language, how the mind in the words keeps changing. A walk by the river is natural, darling, after supper. The air is wet and cool. Clean breezes sweep its stony silence. The woods are just beyond the village and lend their freshness to the air. Beneath the overarching bridge echoes of our laughter merge with liquid murmurings to further open ear. Yes, let's walk down by the river. I want to find some country that Bowles wrote about and call it *natural* like he called us "delicate prey," which is what you get if you don't blink. Man's Natural State troubles my sleep. Last night there were dead fish, responsibilities missed, and trees my neighbor had made part of his house. Otherwise I'm driving always from the back seat downhill through a strange and jumbled city a fast and bumpy wild ride with the accelerator pinned to the floor while I'm blacking out from massive loss of blood. I'll give you your Natural State! Man's first estate is mass suicide. Exit 48. Is the lip on the curb, the urinal's delicate porcelain jaw, the click of the wipers. The canted highway, cats in the dark, air rustling outside in predawn, few cars, inside words, sitting and thinking, getting up to reenlist or take a shit.

approaching storm

dead leaves, some the color of cement if cement were rust, scrape my knees on their way to the grave, buried in gravity, the maple is still full with maple leaves soft as spring, drops begin their pattern on the pond, leaf rustle hath a new inflection, foliate, smallest sunfish leap, dace shimmer, scurry to every edge where arcs lap, cross, fade back into pond, there is no pause, can be no interruption, below words is sound, beneath sound, silence, then dark cacophonies of need, a river swells, above sound are the sounds creatures make to each other by which they are known, above these song, winding all its way into winter, time's valance most acute in the fall where I am over-taken again, there's nowhere to go except in, to listen as babels of rain sweep across the roof in a darkening room

now the morning star

visible from the window, now lost in predawn, be-wildered by light, struck dumb with the drumming of day after day, sodomized senseless by the apparent stupidity of the *populus* of that place, where I find myself, its party in full progress, florescent, titled Yet Another American Century where demands blossom on every bumper, win-dow, face, each unused to ask for anything that it can as easily take, knowing that reach is all, confirming it daily, wary of the indigenous, leery of any man who wears his time too well, except he was another such an idiot as themselves and they could thus assign his favor to an occurrence in the twisted nature of God's Plan: whom the graces seemed to visit first, was a covenant, that they should get theirs in the end—softest saffron dawn just now

sufferin' succotash

beets meatloaf plenty of Campbell's Soup *Reader's Digest Time Life* television lawn snow watches bikes a dog basketball long distance running Phyllis Platt's legs & smile cars plays bird-watching making radios sweet and sour pussy homework bored senseless in every class the halls of junior high impressive after coming from the suburbs of Detroit with their squat notions of a "physical plant" and then in Bowling Green there were alleys & a mind to explore them the pull of graffiti the slightly lost lobotomized look of those born and raised in same place they are currently living especially if that place is small town America awash in drug stores and Christmas displays yet there are some nights dark & deep as any winter where a man kills his wife or a child tortures a favorite pet

do they talk about you? what do they say?

predawn hurricane cattle brawl, how quickly have they passed, those whose lives were made to market, the living which they did each day or so considered while chewing the cud of their culture: constellations of stars, singers and sitcoms, princesses, kings, insane dictators, the talk of nations, pornography, shopping networks, or the lovely *Boy Born without Bones, Sleeps in Bucket* (that's a bold swimmer! I mean, *spermatozoa excelente!* as we used to jeer the apprentice bullfighters with their sheep, until that is the day we witnessed Philipe Gonzages take one apart before our eyes, from roaring mountain testosterone surge to a delicate balance of shimmering despair, dark assertion poised against the desire for oblivion which it shares with the least fly, as Philipe devoured it with his mind

"God Bless America"

(You'd think they'd at least have the decency to use a comma.) On one of those horrifying morning local talk shows, a woman sits on the couch with oxygen tubes still in her nostrils, "I was intensive care for two weeks," she croaks and begins to cry before I can change the channel. Something has scared the shit out of one of my fellow creatures. The trick is to let mind adjust *with the eyes* in the dark. Eliminate the figure. Eno was right, all electronic music has allowed us to hear a single note from an acoustic instrument; whereas the sound from a synthesizer results from the movement of a few atoms, only, amplified, notes from a baby grand involve the vibrancy of billions. What confusions of being, then, in the human forever sounding abeyances of self in the world without?

listening to the rain

knowing what's coming, Lili, a hurricane, might tear *me* a new one this time, landfall by eight, it's quarter-to-five and I'm not sure what I should be doing, thinking of the comedy of consolations, "Good thing I put grandma's bowl in the fridge" as my house floats by, good thing they have a word for it, catastrophic, chaos, wind and rain rake roof (Headline of the Gods!), maybe the consolation of words or music in an expanding room, few trucks on the road, coming home yesterday afternoon, town shutting down, a gleam on every pleasant goddamn thing, on the wheels of shopping carts, sides of cars and buildings, in the eyes of my fellow creatures, friendly, no one frantic, category 3 headed to 4, sharp rain on roof woke me early this morning, already a magnificent beast in the distance

fronted on several

that we might be the lone blue dot in the universe is lovely. the world as a delicately interwoven tissue of events, a binding and unbinding in the connections of the extant, lively present occasion in which the contiguous realities of world and mind, each in unique combination always changing, determine the texture of experience. constellations' spawn. the soul sits in the dark cave of a body and offers sage advice, which body rejects with a spark in its eye indicating the ripeness of its disdain for all things not flesh, not plumed with pulse, a nexus of interlocking and interdependent systems. still cleaning up over two weeks after Lili, still writing about her, thinking. she grew in me, filled my chest with fervor, dark swirl of all around. today a turkey on the way to work.

You kiss like your dad

Imagine a tower built of mountainous windes, ranges over ranges of sheer indifference, unconscious power as mortar of wind and air and water, matter most deeply at odds with itself, tower whose top topples over, plunges off, re-constituted, continually lost and recovered, crazed, what was it I saw in her when I looked?, anything? dark recognition?, nature of fear, granite in mind's socket?, had I ever *seen* a broken tower, for instance?, ever heard its maddening peel across earth, calling us to service our confusions, I had seen blizzards and recognized it there as well, as if it were an eye, or the gleam of an eye like a mind glowing in a coal, grin of white ash, chasms of forgetfulness, absence, mind in granite if granite might be said to have a mind, or the grammar of that gleam.

after Lili

about one family in fifty decides it doesn't mind windows
boarded, no sun to disturb the sacred light of television or
to pollute the ghastly kitchen fluorescents that burn lin-
oleum's pattern, an insane scrabble of black and yellow,
into the stuttering cortex of a brain washed in baths with
chemicals resident in Krispy Kreame, Cheezos, Sara Lee,
& Camels, or maybe they just forget, leave the boards up,
winter's coming anyway, why not live in darkness? why
not? thus, some poor in the country. others are talking
in shopping lines of insurance and tree damage not to
mention everything in the fridge and the freezer which
was of course stuffed with something exotic. While I
grade papers, eat, sleep, wake early, drink coffee, crank up
the computer and write as the house falls all around me.

late autumn

There are words of air and water, elemental as iron and
heavy breathing. We are on a barrel and the barrel is
moving, engaged we say. Words like driving from the
backseat downhill with the accelerator stuck-on-jam
in a strange city. The attentions are bamboo, lively green
shoots, they stand beneath an olive blue sky, or is it *onion*
blue? Has anyone tampered with the controls? No longer
at night, the late popping. Here, coffee is of considered
significance, as is a good shit. It's autumn. I mean in the
fall I never thought would happen. That's a lovely, strange
contraption. A car with little legs and a skirt of banana
leaves. Baboon umbrella. I need serviced immediately.
Mute as planets over my grave, or they are borne on the
backs of dolphins, swimming from an antithetical center.

sign is in the air

crows circle the busted oak, five land, eighteen remain
circling, four more land, two rise, then another takes off
as three more land, all amid squawks in a pattern likewise indiscernible though it seems it *should* make sense
like reading in a dream, the sky a screen, you're stuck
in Reno, in the words a fatal sentence, but maybe something else, again. across your eyes pass planets, epos of
evening ever unfolding night & morning star, were it not
for the rain, septic tank's complaints, and acrid stench of
dying cats. the dead hornet on the sill is a reminder of
something. words have roots that are yet tangled in the
corpse-thick soil of pre-nascent-proto-Indo-European.
for instance, *naught* is no thing, creature, being, not the
dust itself, nor life, and of which nothing can be known.

floating wall

By *suspension* I mean *that weight* by which we listen.
Rain all night, all morning dearly dark, we've abandoned
daylight savings time like a ship that's sinking, deck
running cold, no moon on midnight's waves, the next
moment brushed by sharks on shin. You'd think they'd
have the decency to wait, allow us to adjust. I can't shit
in this house. The septic tank is practicing its gargling
arias in the lower tub and kitchen sink. The roof leaks
and I'm an old man, or I can conceive of being old. How
interesting to live long in time, a floating world gradually
realized as *nothing in remission*. Angels are lead. All
promises off. No more bets. Anyway, I'm already cashed
and the banks are closed for the anniversary of my
death. Ear hovers above the swollen land, water on break.

October,

each morning amid earth's wreckage and continuing
beneficence, birdsong and mosquitoes drift above
debris where webs hang thick with fog, more liquid
than strand on which spiders doze   we are such
beautifully polluted creatures, our dreams run riot with
us, our fears strike us like brutal boys riding pigs, their parents
went to town, might never be back, . . . yet we would love
and *be* loved, have children, would meditate, digest,
conceive *the country from whose borne / no traveler
returns*, puzzled always, yet looking   bury youth in
age, bury the day in my life, dark mountains and streams,
the Rockies marching in dream, Wyoming's sharp but arid
sense of *Who everyone is* and *What's plain stupid* mixed
with the bustier confusions of the Midwest, first the suburbs
and then that other horror, small town America where I
am yet in residence, in a hall, say, fully lit, expectant,
waiting for guests to arrive   a dawn with trucks,
dark cloudbank in the east, nearly purple, no stars but
the waning of night, soft light amid branches, gray
birds   the silences between words and the silences between silences, I was thinking of words this morning in
a sentence, silence as the only thing that lasts after words are
burnt from the mind, from the memory, from dream into silence
this morning in sun's annunciation which enters again
the raucous career of a new world   silence like
the gleam on a drop at the bottom of the mind, beneath a pond, under a lake, an ocean, lit only by the purest
of sources, slightest organic systems, beautiful, lyric
and luminescent   sun rising ever deeper in south's
sink, pointing to winter as though to that which has been
long realized, never considered until confronted, the bare
stupid fact of it, the cold that has entered marrow
having once felt the boney grip of the inexorable, the
gleam beneath the storm   amid the fruits of
harvest, you are full for the moment, satiety is the tree

that grows in the middle of your garden, driving the
Lincoln to town late Saturday, the streets lustrous with
possibility, running on prime, enjoying exactly
the moment, no moment more

Sure Shots

–I want to be an experimental poem.

–*Metaphor for the New Millennium:* Culture as a massive trash compactor, and you were dumped in as it was switched on, then its doors crashed shut, and the machinery wakened from its lubricious sleep, began grinding, and the grinding continues. . .

–The Economics of Skin: You're overdrawn.

–Metal dreams of liquid, liquid dreams of life.

–Language is the mirror we see through.

–from *Definitions for the new Millennium:* Retirement, n. 1. Death's middleman.

–from *Bumperstickers for the New Millennium:* Nothing Succeeds Like Deceit[8]

–from *Exercises in Calculation for the New Millennium:* Chapter 3, Question 14a. A Republican is a failed Democrat. A Republican is what you got after you subtract the human. Delineate in full.

---

[8] The most universal characteristic trait of humanity after self-preservation and procreation of species is not merely the willingness but the slavish desire to be well duped.

Lili, a Hurricane
-for Jerry McGuire and Mark Spitzer, their surge

The story pitches itself one way and then the other, an uncertain pivot. On a white African beach, a child god whispers in turn into the blue ear of the Sky and the green, salty ear of the Ocean, then sits back, toes curled in sand, his face aflutter. Meanwhile Ocean and Sky, after a pause in which they seem to see themselves at last as they truly are, throw themselves at each other, into one another's arms, Sky pressing down, Ocean, opened, up, thrusting back, a brazing of anteriors, as if to prove that they are *not* insane, that their motives are pure, elemental, that any product of their union would be the normal, natural issue of their pouring forth, each into the other, guileless creatures that they are. (It's as though they were born and raised in the Midwest!) Meanwhile their spawn wakens from fetal sleep, and nearly unnoticed amid its parents' proclamations and protestations, crawls forth from spume frothed lips, wet pulsing bulge of Ocean, pudendal arch, amid the sickening rising and falling of pressures, tortuous heaves, emerges backward, breach, already sleek with winds, to the rending of senses, membrane torn from idea, a ripe insanity born to the shrieks of both parents who fall back dismayed, exhausted, then turn bitterly away.

As she rolls across the Atlantic on her heels, she dreams herself a body of storms, a monstrosity, worlds within worlds of air and water and wind: torrents of doubt, fugues of the sheer, winds rising thousands of feet in a few seconds then suicidally throwing themselves off their own cliffs to plunge thousands of feet below, psychotic dervishes, deep unbinding swells (of reference from referents), tumultuous towers, parapets in neural collapse (these result in blind spots), electric spasm in back currents, dark swirl, the black flatulence of eddies, abeyances of thought, little soda jerks running from table to table, cataracts of unholy pleasures, and oh the delicate waterspouts like a ballet of gazelle leaping through the entirety of this infernal tapestry vivant, as through a blazing forest *with the world's on fire*, dancing amid *all hell broke loose*, to a demonic cacophony, a rhapsody *dérangement*, crescendo of blank racket, her brow at 30,000 feet as she slows, stretches and contracts, opens an eye at last, blinks, spies Cuba, and turns, bellowing, to wipe her ass.

Mudslides bury villages, hundreds thought dead, fishermen torn to sea, flash floods, cholera, typhus, diarrhea, infections and so forth. Yet another chance for the United States to remember that *it* is the one that should petition for forgiveness and reach out a hand of generosity and regret. Lost. Death amid the petulance of nations. Death in disregard. Death for its own sake. Stupid motherfucking death!

Fatter by the hour, her howling more bellicose, by turns depressed, morose, plain pissed, her flesh great rolling slabs, gusts up to140 mph, sucking up warm Gulf, farting and kicking and rolling, tearing at her hair, clawing her face, ripping at nipple rings, maniacal laughter, insane cries, the screams of tortured children, choking on her own tongue out of spite (imagine when she gets really mad!), she spots the anus of the nation, lets out an unholy blast, a galloping ass whooop, and even amid the vast chaos of her being–blind fury, tearing off of heads, crystalline farts, all direction forsaken–takes steady aim. Gonna tear us a new one.

Slight breath of air before dawn in the dripping world, fog on the fields, no electricity for over two days, making coffee on the campstove, a French press, chair and two folding tables on the front porch where I have taken residence, eastern rim ringed with rose and roosters' crows, as they say, flinging their curses over a half mile, beautiful eerie cock before dawn mixed with bird song, a car every now and then, end of another night's curfew, St. Landry Parish, dusk to dawn, crickets a constant and the humming grind of a generator in the distance, writing by lantern light (where I began!), cattle bawl, crows, and a series of shotgun blasts no shit as I write this to the southwest, someone's taken care of the wife and kids, even the cockroach smiles as it passes to the door, just now, this just breaking, the tip of sun's head like a giant cock, massive glowing coal beneath treeline, nudges its inexorable way into the cunt of a new day, and into the longest running dream of the world.

As she approaches Marsh Island, nightward, she outdoes herself in fury, tornados racked with rain, garroting gusts, gaspings, buzzsaws half-a-mile across, broken off, slung through storm, flung earthward, blasts of boat burst, prodigious death rattle, unthinking hatred ratcheting upwards ever flinging herself down upon any sign of ground, any molecular stability, pretense of cohesion, shards of winds barreling through matter (even the electrons are aware of her presence!), as all manner of thing is made several, and to drift in her passage. Thus, landfall.

The following morning the stupid chewing hysteria of the populous was as palpable as Gulf air, fat fucks fighting at five o'clock, lining up to buy generators at over five hundred dollars a pop. People running them inside their houses so they won't be stolen by others of their filthy kind. Juice junkies. Over twenty CO_2 poisoning cases at local hospitals. Nurses pulling double shifts. Emergency crews doing what they must. Some men traveling over seven-hundred miles to help restore electricity, sleeping in their trucks. Some women cooking everything in their freezers and taking it to friends, two families in one house. Insurance adjusters torn from living rooms across the South. And when the storm was full blast, kids running down the street, one man raking, another ripping shingles off his house, another standing in wonder (*here you are*). Many will miss trees that they'd grown to love in years to come. How to think it? One woman died running a generator in her kitchen. Another little exercise in natural selection? Some tableau too rich for comedy, too stupid or pathetic for the tragic stage? The beginning of fall? Simply change of season? Once more, our mongrel existence. And of myself? Extreme middle condition.

She closes her eye, tilts her head, and pushes in, over twenty-seven-thousand cubic miles of maniacal fury bearing down on this land, thrashing the shit out of Intercoastal City, Perry and Henry, her hair thick with the fire of screams, snarl of hellish birds, screech of jackals, torture of small beasts, old women, the grinding of grinders, cries at the other end of working bone-saws, sounds for which no ear was made, this giant deaf bellowing bitch of wind and water, cloudwall, chasms of air, now a dark, unrelenting force bearing down on Abbeville, Kaplan, Leroy and Rayne, as she puts her shoulder into it, Scott, Lafayette, feeling the resistence of land as a burning through her lower fifth, up to mid-calf, it feels like having skin blasted off by sand, begins as irritation, rises quickly through the sacred stages of consciousness to her full and ready attention, and it makes her, finally . . . mad!, lashes at Iota and Maxie screaming fucking hatred spitting out signs trees poles roofs pets small cars mobile homes pitched like sick jokes over the yard, life's debris!,[9] crud pasted on every surface, leaves, pieces of carton, clippings, winds over everything there is to name, she smacks Church Point a good one, and another, another, a stampede of trumpets, tornados shooting out of her sides, now tortured barrels, like flaming brands, all matter of manner under ripe terror, interrogation, opposing appositives as well, she looks out over what is left of her right shoulder–in her rage she has not realized how far the burning anguish has advanced–toward Sunset, spies a figure in a pasture, head bare, face up (addressing her), she pisses a warm blast in his direction and presses on, now feeling the burning at her neck, JesusGod!, begins kicking with all her might, tears off body parts, flabby gusts and torques of wind, sends them scattering, Richard, Eunice, Mamou, but the burning has entered her brain like a wall of fire crossing the room, from which a crescendo ascends, beckoning, . . . and she is a lost aria, forgetting herself.

Almost a week later, electricity happily restored, the world still looks like happy shit, corners of disarray wherever one turns, signs have new careers as modern dancers, trees lift their shirts of grass and dirt to show their naughty parts, what do torn homes show?, everyone now carries a story or two that will nicely fit with everyone else's, each aware that his or her piece has a short shelf-life, except for the few whose suffering was disproportionately greater, or who had some tale of being drunk, falling asleep, only to wake when the truck was lifted (and he fouled his pants), but for the rest, their stories stale after a few weeks and the only time they'll think of Lili thereafter is when filling out forms, or rebuilding a porch or roof, replacing a mobile home, or missing the stance of a favorite oak, perhaps for its meditative value, but by then they'll only remember a shadow of her malice, simply an *occurrence of their past*, another carnival when they all shared something they can barely recall the fullness of, their measure for, her pure magnificent fury, yet for three or four of their fullest hours, all the most important things in their lives had a new center upon which to pivot, this was Lili.

As she travels north she widens, hammered softly down and out like an old song, an amnesia of storms, brows of towering cloudwalls shrunken to

---

[9] How will it look, with each of us, our end?

stumps and shrubbery on a gray field, Little Rock, Memphis, the massive resistance of land, trees and hills, sheer distance, slowing as she goes, always north, and north she peters out, Evansville, Terre Haute, a mindless abbreviation of her former self, up the Mississippi, the Ohio, a rainy day, spoiling weekends, watering early winter crops, widening the valleys a drop.

Or

-second alternate for Pisces

To say that your later years will be unfortunate constitutes a criminally crude understatement for the screaming horror you'll find. For centuries, people will tell your story to explain what "hell on earth" might actually mean, and their listeners will never be able to forget a single, fucking word. Your fate will be so alien and strange that no drop of empathy shall be shed by even the dewest of youth when witnessing the miserable end of your life. No balm will attend your name to a lonely, forsaken grave. Do you *want* this for yourself, Pisces? Can't you think of a better way? Before it's too late?

ℑ ⋯ ◇ ρ ∮ ∤ ℰ ≑ ∟ℛ≳, if then, not

Never is not now though she fuck you all
ways & twisted into tomorrow like an Irish
toothache you wake up fucking go to bed
fucking as well if not better than ever
before each time is like to blow your
brains out icky sticky over the door
and over all her several surfaces, never
is not now, and always was.

Time slips beneath the wheels as though we are driving as we always are into late autumn to extend what we've discovered of the expansive, border-crashing green on all hands, liquid swirl of satisfaction beyond mute satiety of need as natural state of man, yet deeper into time-come-what-must, of measure most meagre, diet of winds and rain, smacked by the world, a flat fish on the face of our eye.

The body unlearns itself, drains itself of limbs, leaches marrow from strength, waking old, thrashing through another day, or like the man lives in a shack, head not nearly so hard as stone, yet he is set, against it, ridge for a pillow, or he is *for* it, lumber of his life, all the hammers and pens, both house *and* epic. In the end you have your hands, and your heart, and your head, and your dick. That's it.

I was young once, a poet as you are, perhaps, if you are, perhaps, a poet, or if you are young, as I was once (no palindrome intended), a rental house on the bitter side of Columbus, working class, a copy of the *Cantos* (twice read), & an eye for the sunsets of that drear place, days driving into winter, bitter mute prospect even for youth. Likely you might find yourself in a similar situation. What do you do?

No reason to get all dressed up just to jack off, he said, it's come-as-you-are, or I've missed you, *where have you been* (don't ever leave again, okay? No reason for reason but deeper this season into living, wake to what's missing, fall asleep to measure what will never return, that we might find ourselves in the absence of, given to its orders, where recognition shimmers, a blind sheet over oblivion.

Dayspring. Window faces east over cattlefield, treeline, and into morning's bright estate, transport, crossing the Atlantic thru pitch of storm, and onto evening's continent where, at this precise latitude, in the backroom of a house, a boarded-over porch, someone is dying in a foreign language, hovering, as source opens beneath his cot, so rich is life for us, each, drifting into the dance of a single ending.

"Except for what it does to you, death ain't all that bad, especially if you don't mind the smell." He's laughing. It's later. Age's cousin has arrived from another party, some little fanfare. He's well *greezed* already, shiny, making himself obnoxious with that tongue, holding court in the den. He's got his eye on *every-* thing, he says, glancing up, as though *you'*d understand. There's only one room.

someone is shouting at night from inside an ice-fishing shed, mid lake, rhythmic and insistent, the great houses mute blotches against bank, merged in tree, barely absences on mute spectral whiteness, in the shed, now a translucent scrim, a single light throws monstrous shapes across walls &, most ominously from within, over a low ceiling, the screaming makes no sense to the observer, yet he wakes to it

dearth of cicadae, treefrogs, crickets, and the great bulldozers late evening into night, such songs of love and might have long since left their sense behind, echo fading into a land crammed on summer's overbirth, where a quietus gathers them, thick with stupor, body-urge toward oblivion, dark compulsion in the heart of every blooming thing, death inscribed inside the crown of each seed's skull

What mind in the wind, dark rain, this road & evening, huddled in the branches, just beginning to starve, the sick, the frail, old, ill and enfeebled all seem to acknowledge it with a precision many of us may come to know *if we're lucky*, as they say, in the distant future, pointing somewhere with their brows, somewhere other than here. Yet beneath this season's glower they don't seem so damned sure.

silence, spun of abandonment into thick cords of oblivion, dark roots, amnesia's tentacles, the fibrous hush after caress, absence, and the shuttling thread of everything lost to everyone, including animals, insects: home, heart, purpose; which web, woven, catches us while the tight net of matter relaxes, opens, & we slip thru to such a silence as though we've never known *any*thing, ever before

occasionally something is witnessed so odd or horrific, that words can only crowd like cattle at the rails, stupid & dull, as they go whirling past, with what such rupture in sightstream, mindstream, to rolling stock in liquid memory that it might find purchase, perch within our lives like carrion birds or birds of prey beneath the ribs watching every movement's furtive moment, a pair of claws at eye's bottom

Not even mid-January and the grackles are back, cacophonous song just after sunset, then again a half hour before dawn, when they hush, begin their clucking, silent by comparison, & fly out, wave after wave by the thousands into a new day. Has spring so early come, winter left behind? What the fuck's going on? One day a man walks into a lake, another blows his heart out his back. Into what distance?

Portrait de une femme

Thou art a paper bag, stuffed with feces, a mouthful of fresh excrement. All of your life you have been proud of your ignorance and mental sloth. You'd as soon scratch as think. You'd rather fuck than either. Truth be known, only fucking and eating make any sense to you. Maybe flattery, but you wouldn't know; you're so wretched that even the most down-on-his-luck sycophant has passed you by. Besides, you have nothing to offer. Unless he has an exquisite notion of the perverse, anyone who would even *think* of screwing you as an act of gratification is not worth consideration, even in passing. Rain on the roof this morning.

Swollen Mirror

Eyes look into face beyond
recognition, you are who you
see, we say, beneath which you are
nothing, an empty sack of
pretenses, a whine, a settledness
in your ear, and a scratch beneath
that, the swollen bite becomes in-
fected, in the story everybody dies,
nothing to be made whole again
like bread, take, eat, survive in the
emptiness of sole condition, now
look into your eyes, deep inside is a
prisoner undergoing monthly interrogation, wet hoses and knives, no
sleep for days, none for days before, a ruin falling in on itself, a bad
beginning, a stupid middle, and a
terrible fall by way of end. Have
a nice fucking day!

Or

The possibilities are finite
but beyond our knowing.[9]
Certainly our being is constrained
by time and place, but not even prisoners
know their limits. The barrel is left open
at the top that we might see clouds cross
and contemplate the blue and gray or the
net of stars across which planets

                              glide,
night after night, that we would tell
stories of their passing, shore unto shore. Can
we live in our own lives for once?, and if once,
how not always? Is this what you've feared? To be
swallowed by direction? Like the serious. What
it might come to be in its observance? You
think about such things.

---

[9] Mayer.

Sure Shots

-You would become not just a poet but a great poet by spending less time learning your craft than an apprentice butcher spends learning his? (Paraphrasing Pound) Are you exempt from the laws of human physics? How interconnected do you consider the brain and the mind? Deeply? (from *A Calculus for the New Millennium*)

-Bumpersticker for the New Millennium (rear end of car stove in): Physics's a bitch!

-Tractor-Trailer Trapped in Traffic (Another Headline of the Gods? . . . or a Sticka for All Occasions?)

-Don't botch your senility.

-from *Blurbs for the New Millennium*: Only half steps from oblivion.

-from *Definitions for a New Millennium*: **shock** *n*. 1. A realization like being bitten behind the ear by a rat, a gigantic rat, behind ear and crisply into spine or brainpan, and you're still alive and know that she's lugging you back to a hungry nest, and you think, *at least I can't feel anything*, but your eyes . . .

-I want to be the guy who gets to write everything.

That is.

If sighs be songs, then farewell goes out
singing. Yesterday's love is gone. How clear.
Moat in the eye widens. Fate does a jig in the
wings. You can't remember your name much
less your lines. You've all but forgotten you
were in a play. Fate glides into cat walk and curl
amid the standard six-step, his face rippling
with laughter. Perhaps. And yet there is, always,
another, I would see her . . . better. I would
what I would. Is there trace to follow, hint of
welcome most melodic in distance, soft seeds
of light dancing down trail that it might open
onto a clearing, a meadow, or maybe a country
radiant with tolerance . . . why not a continent?

What information which in its loss we might call ourselves forgiven, if not forgot.

I spent a few minutes on that sentence. It starts itself a jumpy little melody, staircase rhythm, defers it, then picks it back up, setting itself softly but certainly down like a teacup at a flea market. I'm also surprised how quickly it happens for such a gangling thing. It's all arms and legs coming down to breakfast. It's actually kind of a dud. A firecracker that doesn't go off. Maybe the fuse smolders. How speak of such a thing?

A few notes the morning after Republican victories

Wet as Midwest spring, profuse as her
summer. Two wedges of geese, one small,
one large, streaming to the northeast,
waving white in the wind. . . .Where will they
winter? A month after the hurricane, still
there is rot in all the crevices and over most
surfaces. Azaleas shudder in the bright
air. The sky an anemic blue, almost
white at the horizon. A few small clouds.

Still Monday still

before dawn and I'd like to write about
one cup of coffee, the first, but it's gone
or down to the last few tepid sips, gully
washers. Had I wanted to consider such
pleasures, as thus the cup I had, as dumb,
beautiful servants, forever young, who would
bend their dainty wills to mine and always
keep their twats shaved? Something like
that. Still Monday, still before dawn. ♪

anvil blows

rain between rains this morning more rain more water on ground, great day for the nightmare of waking once more into your own life, the self you hold in your arms like an unruly child, otherwise *the condition*, of living and leaving at once, like everyone else, what light beneath such darkness? what have you had to accept to be *with* yourself? who *else* do you hold? truly, & so forth, days durable, nights soaked in dream, life leaking through your body, your self wavering in middle distance or a form that goes before you, always, how will you look in dying? set against what hillside flowering in winter, what reversal in the hard current, four ages of man: love, work, regret, and death, set into the inexorable forward motion of the universe, what luminescence in balance?

instrumentation of the arbitrary

he enters a world in which everything is put on *different*, the eyes of the girl on back of the man, no surface with edge narrow enough not to take us in, warm mouth of the moment, chewed and swallowed to an emptiness not un-familiar by far, like *being* without *me* in it, its darkness articulate, its caverns rushing with thought, or currents that so resemble thought they curl back upon, entangle themselves, tie themselves in knots, then rush forward from *r* to *w*, fall *l* into *p*, rhythm bounding back off walls, vastness of inner space, a world sometimes there, . . . sometimes not, without measure, who can tell?, then what would it mean to be certain of just one thing, one mark set sure in life's flesh, the letter of a single fact?

there's one season, only,

winter, bare bone on desert floor, not even the memory of meat, and to have lived among juices, what was that?, rumor of feathery life long gone since, urge of growth in seed head, languorous exchange of green, cicada as portal to evening's meditation, all buried in fetal sleep, as though they'd never been, sweet descent as consolation, pitch beyond knowing, floor beneath conception, finality without cause, yet one would dream, as bone would wrap itself once more in storied flesh, would *do it over again* only this time without the interference, the bad ass dam breaks, confusions, cataleptic abyss, you can almost see it rise before you, a presence *in the midst*, and straighten, stand, or rotate as a planet, perhaps a reason to have been living all along, but when you reach for it, it's gone.

Yes,

in the wind, in the rain this morning, and why not? in all the branches, sky reaches down to us a happy hand, blue and helpful, maybe, as the balloons of our youth sail onto rivers of air that are age. What*ever* did you think? They put you in a monkey suit and shoved you out the door, a bit abrupt for reflection. And then the jumping around began as the mind kicked in, banging the bedpan on the brainstem, and on the bedstand. Holy tantrum. Unlovely life buckled in. *No*, as a look pounces on its face. Life, a disgraceful affair of crime and circumstance, or time and distance. You ride dark bubbles of thought, brutal shapes that break on the surface, scorching desert and plain with the volcanic insistence of words. Or maybe the gods got something right for once in your life. What are the odds?

caught in the cross-hairs of the headlights,

the small animals bear down with all their lives, staining our asphalt gardens with their dear selves, thoughts and liquid centers, *it's a long way where we're going, might as well catch a ride*, juiced up frog on a rainy Saturday night, possum with his worm bouncing out and about, armadillo between the blind pleasures of a hog (nothing personal), even the skunk is sore amazed (this is a birthday poem!) as the sacred equations of physics which have been running all along, mainly in the background, sheer speed and mass, light and blinding weight, wind up for yet *another final demonstration,* . . . what *is it* to so surely *mean*? and is it *against, in lieu of* the rough exteriors as you find them, *a burlesque of cooperation*, or you, yourself, the actual, brute stare bearing down?

Death blossoms in oblivion

Each petal, soft as silken purse to thumb, returns the luster of darkness beneath hammered gold, the stare in eye, each whispers your nearest name, and is then silent. Cars and trucks round the curve into deepest winter's night (I woke wondering what is it, that rush I heard, the wind! What does my father hear just this side of that which opens to exclude him? Scorpioidal cyme, the *whole inflorescence* curved on itself, like space, both there and not there, where he sits beneath its pitch of sheer, takes nothing in. Shims between a golden door and unfurling of oblivion. Or takes in every blessed thing, his face a screen, reflection, an empty basket. Death shuffles the deck again and again. He never seems to tire of his stupid joke. Has all the living globe as audience, attentive.

free rain

would we have an alphabet of flowers and flames, notion
of sheer as falls off falcon's wing, stoop's onrush of air
that paralyzes prey, wall-shattering distances in middle
ear, letters forged like leaves on autumn's air, blistering
with color, acidic light bleaching the sky more each day
with advent of winter, deepest night, drained of all but
stars, haunted by Orion, a bewilderment of constellations
inhabits each stroke, in the wrist of every eye a graven
image, script in which each word's a wave cast into a
world of waves, leaves ticking cold, wide night air
of the actual, where all else matters, punctuation like
ships rocking in their berths mid-storm or a horse in its
stall as flames fall upon upwending horsy screams, just
for the shining in our brain, wonder of coldest predawn

frost

crisps rot, the dead beast bristles once again, merely
a hiccup in the infinite winter of his non-existence?,
perhaps, where is any point the center, whose circle is
everywhere?, *it is the mind creates the finite* (oh is it?),
solely singular for the singleness, the self who would for
others do but this, is dipped in frozen swamp, staked out
to wait the dawn (it's going to be a long night!), why not
shoot the elves and eat the buggers raw?, cold rock in its
mind, the yard a frozen crust of pie, blossom as zero left
to burn, camilla petals curling into ripe oblivion, locks
rot in fallen fruit, we are gas at core, in our lively corpse,
or nothing if not noxious fumes and wayward eye, a cave
of echoes, friendships, loves, whatever was begotten,
lost, coma at the center of the earth, & this its silent sign

even when

flap of bird's wing, silk wave laps shore then retreats in
suck of sound, soft inhalation, prolonged waiting, that is
we're only waiting . . . , would we ride the crest of moment's movement if we could?, we would do so gladly,
simple as that, logic as clear as what's *behind* the mirror
(or do I mean *beneath*?), maybe I mean the *concept* of
identity, moon as mirror of prose, both here and not, state
defined as the absence of all others, looking over its
shoulder, at whatever it is stands there, before us, someone's impending death, the house is on fire, or morning's
fog, dripping even as it gathers to resolve into a day as
yet another in the world which we ignore at our peril,
though it seems so worthy ignorance, the inanity of the
populus, dissolution, and the crude irreversibility of time.

some bodies should never be repeated in the Dawn[10]

some are attracted to light. some unfold in music or
lust. some given to food, danger, the dark satisfactions,
a basin in their mind where vermin spawn like words to
infect their every thought, grotesques, ideologues, sheer
opportunists, confused and dumb, and everywhere fear
scorching the cranium, like a blowtorch the temple of its
latest victim, blind revulsion sprouting tongues, lathered
at the wheel. others given to river and cloud, tumult of
buildings, towering falls, the peregrine on patrol, sirens
and horns tumbling down valleys, walls of voices in
evening sky, conversations of insects, and mist softening
light of foothills. such conceptions, dancers themselves,
disappear into their referents under time's slightest brush
or breath. perhaps grace is nothing if not stepping aside.

---

[10] Lorca

burial of caves

Saint-Saëns saw a sea in his sleep. Dropped in a key. Since he'd visited a zoo only that day (trying to win the favors of one slight puff, some thirty years his junior), his dream threw up the stuff of tigers, a twirling crock, one bird's full throated, *Barely dying yet, boss*, crest stiff in morning, rigor of the quick (she stirs?) music is always right in middle of (definitely indefinite), where surface turns, blinks, swirls with what's moving to edges (likewise indefinite), always (if listening). That is, sweet caves she had & all her caves gave way to caverns, each a life renewed, a *site* wherein to bathe existence in the waters of her oblivion. Saint-Saëns forgot all about the animals, & his music disappeared into night sky, into ranges of her air, the soft light of her eyes, & into all her tangled being.

And in the end there's no end but forgetting[11]

begins shredding plans, then desire to plan. future gone, it devours past. memories dim in shade, darken, cast a burnished sheen against the pit, and then are gone, as though they'd never been. saves present for last, all but the very moment on which you float, a circular plain, billowy period on its back, thank god you fit. it's infinite. there's not even water below. no distance. like slowly e-rasing yourself til you disappear or discover a pattern beneath the scribblings of what's-going-on-right-now. but everyone's someone else again and all you got left are your obsessions, and the pain. yellow of parrot's beak. woman's claw. animals in her neck. running savanna of flesh. what's she sitting on is *gone*. you continue. 'til you don't. what hole at the end of descent? what whiteness?

---

[11] Mayer

Sure Shots

–Generic ending: Der Tod, perched on windowsill of world, crows at dawn, and all horizons echo.

–Another Title for the New Millennium: *Sure Shots*, with a Blurb for the New Millennium: "Emergency text for next to can. For anything from shitting-feast to a few black bbs, you can't beat it. Elastic, it will fill your drawers with warm, ball-hugging joy. You will chuckle in the mirror as though you understood what you just read. Don't forget to wash."

–What are the differences between imposing and finding a line on a blank page, drawing, writing without the imposition of words, but as though leaning *to* a future seconds in advance, or throwing balance forward, with faith in ear and faint but full anticipation, that they will find you before you have to go looking for them, and as always the discovery is ripe as is recognition, as is the line on the page. I have a hard time thinking about it without considering it a presence.

Morning Memory Raga

Burgundy darkness, plants stretched across. Leafwork, red wine. In his dream, he pulls himself off the floor of sleep and goes walking. Down corridors, sidewalks and into hills, etc. An idea follows him. Why must he come to his errors like a whipped dog, ashamed for what he did, and frightened, but willing to suffer the punishment of his life in order to bask once again in He Whose Presence such resolution may be found, what peace or what is it, asleep in the warm lap of experience? Restitution. Thirty-seven beautiful freshmen begin caressing him with their eyes. They are tasting his every port and portal. Yikes! He tells a small group, "but I probably couldn't stand to talk to one of them for more than fifteen minutes. Not more than three in a single day." Someone from beyond asks him to sign a chair, her husband doesn't mind. He signs for them both, not realizing his mistake until later, when he wakes, unmated. In the darkness, leaves and the scroll of eyes, the desolation of planets woven into landscape, hard plain at night, desert where his hand makes a curious talisman. If you get rid of all the swaddle, it says, you could get on with your life. Shining in the darkness, perplexed, amused, he falls back down, and fast asleep.

a very man per se, and stands alone

sun stumbles thru fog this morning
   after last night's rains,
        mirror green, grass glows
  in late haze
      with singular intensity
           as though thought
    descends . . .
       an ape wonders at his own curiosity
  or an orangutan "fixes" his call in the elegiac
   after seeing what he saw, on one such
          morning you might wake to realize
     you've never meant anything, that all your relations
         are based on a notion
           you had once walking down the stairs
   at your parents' house:
          always pretend an upper hand
            exaggerate your position

    and while you're wondering why this
      doesn't seem to bother you, a
      car horn starts barking
        sharp intervals
          in your ear . . .
            C'est l'alarme!

ad perpendiculum columnas

Heat rises as wedge of fog across pond
one foot above the surface on the northern bank
to over fifteen feet on the southern, moving upward in
slightest breeze, I cannot even feel in memory
sun broken
into bars and beams   through trees
woods into words
–chinese tallow, tupalo gum,
pine and maple
to fill the thought of poems
like
cattle brawl to the southeast
dogs in northeast, birds to the west and
north-
west, & a woodpecker to the north pour into
the face of morning. . . .
(I should be
so exact

A Hell

as Pound's, where nobody knows they're *here*, not *there*, or as if *we* were, packed tightly in crevices of our loathsome selves, hiding as eels beneath cliffs of coral, basting our balls at Vulcan's flue in ocean's basement, or in an ancient Studebaker at the bottom of a bay, a skeleton whose feet have slipped their cement its (our) only companion. Good night. Fast asleep. Tender sheathe beneath tons of water, boulder over boulder crushing mind in its shelter, newly hatched nebula in apodal skull, a tiny hut on the veldt, vast open cavern of everyday life, who knows what will happen next?, better cling to *this* miserable existence than tempt another, calculations soft as butter on bee's wing, replete with honey cakes each morning of the world we forgot to remember ourselves (absolutely!), just what it is we're doing (what *are* we doing?), banked in flourescents, a cataleptic strobe, the mind astutter, who cares?, dire blackouts flooding spillways, entire circuitries going down, cloacal furnaces spewing forth moral sensibilities awash in the brine of relationships, so-called, and mortality, our sense of scale blasted from the cranium by television, the mind a slave to the dialectical machine's ubiquity, memory a little button that doesn't work anymore except when the vehicle's cold, and it's cold as hell!, always, thus frozen, buried beneath onslaught of ice, remembrance's freezing slush, upending tons of water, cliffs of guilt as ocean bearing down, pressure lines of scroll work at edge's eye cracks like glass, racket ratcheting, friction of self against barely yet-conscious existence, the sheer burning intensity, and we're always back where we didn't even want to begin in the first place, as they say, all over again. No figures to follow, no guides, ropes, potions or spooky alembics, no interview with the gore-besotted, unhappy dead, those who have at least arrived at the consolation of a single truth, the one mistake of their lives, existence, which replicated, grew, and for which . . . etc., seen through the ridiculously bright lenses of anguish and remorse, brought into excruciating focus, delineation, and alignment. Maybe they don't know where *they* are either, or remember who they are. Or our feet have come free from that which constrained them, now they can roam as we can, about the cab, flow through the deep, icy flush of fevered existence, water colder and deeper than pressure can bear and where fish still peck at our pretty bones out of lovely, lonely reflex. Yes, hell's an ocean where light's swallowed by greed of depth, water's for openness of spirit above the thickening mist into which we drop, foul and frigid, thus numbed to a child, to a dop, the self reeling

136

enters an alley, cortex wretched and writhing with shadows, misshapened forms, bruised will beyond intent and overblown, without proportion, no part unto part informed by measure of certain thought or mind's deft motion, an underwater cinema soundless beneath the crush of weight and lesser diversions, the sordid pageant squirming across the national stage, so meagre and apparent it's a wonder anyone will ever call it *history* someday. . . much less *our history.* A more pathetic bunch to run a nation I can't imagine. Not this nation. Maybe some little hell-hole beneath Indonesia saturated in the karma of Dripping Lizard and Papa Pia Secundo. When everyone finds out that Numb Nuts has been jerking off the whole time, get ready. Expect no mercy from our enemies. Prepare to see our soldiers smoked alive and eaten on al-Jazeera, rappaz will sample their screams, and the U.S. will further unbind itself from the nations which believe they might become both increasingly modern *and* civilized (i.e., humane), that given the conditions and tacit encouragement, their citizens might live to speak directly, see clearly, think, and sprout wings to rise above the sludge and offal of the meagre human-rapacious-kinde and into what upper elements they can. A Hell in which heart and hand have come to nothing less than zero, where a majority of adult males would rather see someone falling down a staircase than a traffic jam.

In this sneaky pit we find ourselves, loosening from Europe (who now must take advance). We wake to it once and again each morning when we open television (which is what, by the way, to our attentions? Where is the serious when an admiral's put in charge of gathering information on every citizen, only most of *them* have not been convicted of five felonies. Criminal intent saturating the mentality of the executive branch, the Pentagon, not to mention all political appointments including and especially the chief political advisor, traitors to consciousness in cabinet positions, departmental heads, wooden ideologues appointed to the judiciary, knobby-minded creatures blaring this nation's ripe goodness to the world, the quasi-literate dense with radiospeak, unconsidered opinions, in short "Condition Human Spam" all twisted and made afraid of their very nature, unless it's constituted as some green at in a dark lounge in Jersey with a deer over the bar and a Bud waterfall. It's an ugly sick sad fucking thing we've made of it and if we're the last chance, good riddance, as Jeffers said.

secum aliquid

softest hint of salmon beneath gray-blue fog before dawn, cloudbank
low on eastern horizon under mullion, a few azalea stems, and the
remainder of summer's canopy, leaves, some limbs still limp in
their sockets from the storm, one pine bough yet hangs from a
river birch, twenty feet distant, as sun's head emerges in the east-
south-east, no way that there's only 23.45 degrees between sun's
rising at either solstice, surely this sway rivals the heart's on *its* pen-
dulum, tolling through seasons of leaf, weed, and stony rubble, days
and nights, the four ages of man, its arc traversing ours, as up a slope,
narrow trail hugging mountain, it stops, moves neither north nor south,
where way is steepest it turns, and the silhouette of its presence, luminous,
sears a bloody tattoo onto mind's retina, a warning?, or crossing?, as sun
climbs from cloudbank into cloud above it, where it is swallowed whole,
to reemerge some minutes later, a hard yellow glow, heaviness on the lids.

for Tim

Now you know more
than I'll know ever
in this life
of death.

no wiser and worse for the wear

the possible leans in a doorway,
his back to you,

you are in a chair,
in the room,

beyond the silhouette of his form,
plains shimmer in the hard summer's day,

the room sounds like just after loud music,
he shifts his head, a shoulder,

you are trying to draw his face
from memory,

he whistles,
you take another drink

all the time and today

"Now I have vertigo all the time and today, January 23, 1862,
I suffered a strange warning. I felt pass over me the wind of
imbecility's wing."
        –Baudelaire

How will it feel in passing? Bright and cold as a chill flashes
across my father's eyes, or as though they punctured your
spinal cord and are pumping in pure helium? What
nerve, exposed to light, shimmers in pain? Bright
dance of sensation. Yellow wall in Mexican courtyard.
Tincture of whore's smile. Green lost in eye-glint. Your
thumbnail's telling the tablecloth about Father Christmas,
he hadn't heard about the loss of all functions, soiling living
rooms of the nation, he didn't know about the spontaneous
masturbation sessions, in malls, ringed with elves, a writhing
wreathe. I think I'm getting in the spirit of the season and it's
only Thanksgiving, bright shawls and baskets on the horizon of
saying-something-of-moment as syllables pour out in ropey vomit-
like strings, or ben-wa balls, or maybe it's the spirit's gotten into me.

He laughed on the day of his birth and lived in the wilderness on cheese

Nearly three millennia ago, he stood on a bridge between the old world and this, of which he remains the beginning. Behind him, a pre-history stuffed with spirits (turn over an old log), haunted by their whisperings, and with their shoutings in the middle of the head; fierce elements, implacable, speaking languages of desert and wind, the mountains riddled with prophets; highway men on all trails, nomads and hoards, cattle thieves; the eternal law of nature, a melody of winds, flames, waves, all crashing; perhaps a time when each gesture had an outside, only (softest rose of predawn just now), where when you sang to yourself, you were someone else, the dew was fresh each morning, and children hung in all the branches like delicious fruit. Before him, the separation of elements, invention of nothing, tearing the world apart; classification of song; the press; beasts sprouting demi-logic, "commentators"; all manner of thing regardless, this strange contraption, a culture on the back of which history, itself a horse, rides, as on a flatbed of a runaway train. Yet our mountains still ring with song, our trees are also softest at dawn and dusk, always, and we wake at night to a sort of silence as well, though we rarely hear voices in our heads. (I heard one, once, as clear as daylight say, "You know better than that," . . . and I had to admit. Others are often almost just on the cusp of my not nearly hearing quite, quiet, beside my own, of course, which I have never heard. All this from the donkey's mouth. Wondrous beast!) Nearly three millennia ago, he was a wedge between that world and this. A golden shim.[12]

---

[12] Origin unknown.

Change of Habits: A Mini-Essay
-for the New Coffee Machine

I would like to know just exactly how *observance* went from a perceptual to a practical act, the physical delicately woven as substance into the psychological, cultural, religious, and familial history of the present. I understand the French are to blame for this as well. Actually in his purity Confucius could have made such a move (he was liquid!), the world "seemless," gullies and streams without metaphor, reservoirs and oceans, all as *actual* as we are, or the river, a dream of a life in which he moved (slow motion calligraphy) with certain sense, *How can there be vulgarity when the noble-minded is present?* Appearances disappear . . . and you realize where you are. Already here. Fronting the first dark rain of winter, each year, for instance, remembering its contemplative valences, the metal in its throat, light of instant, watched, addressed, revered for what it was of the world, and of you, of what it might become. Observances remind us *who* we are. Who are we? Propel us outward, beyond our densities. Pink, sprindged cross dirt on window panes, turns sudden orange.

Sure Shots

–   Letters move in lit-
      tle waves. Spooky isn't it?
            I don't give a shit.

–Frank Stanford's *The Battlefield Where the Moon Says I Love You* is a
damned fine ride. Though never thrilled with his short work, I always
suspected his canvas might be the long work, and that's where his energy
and verve pay off. Imagine putting a camera on the front of a run-away
locomotive, an iron bull full of steam and beam careening thru memory,
steel, sweat, and vision, nightmare fishing stories, bad blood, The World's
Smallest Man, etc., barreling down steep mountain passes, slipping the
tracks, to leap . . . and fall . . . tumbling . . . (film still rolling) . . .think how
beautifully awkward a train in its ripe concession to gravity, now think how
to structure the film *while* you're still shooting, trappt with the crew five
cars behind the engine following the long desperate arc down in slow
motion; i.e, don't sweat the edit, just get it in the can.

--From *Definitions for the New Millennium*: **literal**, adj. 1. What the
word believes it says. (Usage note: Think prior to application.)

–The Future Doesn't Exist. (Sticka for an anti-teleological association or
for a hedonist society?)

–Writing exercise I can't assign: While writing, when you feel yourself just
beginning to loosen up or it begins *going slack*, stop, make yourself hot, get
to the point to where you're ready to strip and toss off, . . . then go back,
and continue writing.

bright occasion by which we listen

who is it inhabits the ear, finds it fit
habitation, abode in which to consider
what is, was, what may be again,
and what maybe never was as well . . .
but if he falls from that ear down onto
the cement, how many stories?, clawing
at building's skin, suffocating inrush of air
before impact, frantic bones wedded to
rock, then given to the mute chemical
processes, movements of landscape, only,
geography, or if he is swallowed by the mind,
leviathan, a blossoming of ocean or its
evagination, streaming destruction, pockets
of air gasping for breath, ribbons shattered in
its passing, heart of waves stoppt, what
silence?
       how sound him, he who is without
measure? (*who* is without measure?), what
bell in the distance, radiant wave of air within
air, sinuous, round, itself a bell, might
bring him to himself, wavering, the Indo-
European root for *homunculus* is **dhghem-**, for
instance, *earthling, groom of the world,* bright
distinction still shimmering in an orchard mid-
morning, or what was it the voice said to you in
your head?, he who you've always known, telling
you what you already knew (for how long?), plumb, line
under wave, submerged yet poised, stance certain, rock
of the world in his heart, obsidian, dark giving back
the dark, his recognition always sudden, certain.

solstice two days out

```
f                  r                   o                      m
h                   e                  r                      e
w               h           e              r                  e
l        o          n          g             e                r
w           o          r              d                       s
a                      r                                      e
e         a         s           i              e              r
t                                                             o
r                  e                   a                      d
w               h           e              r                  e
o                           d                                 d
w           o          r              d                       s
e                  v                   e                      n
w                  a                   v                      e
```

solstice two days out, take two

```
w                  a                   k                      e
o                                                             n
t                           h                                e
b           r               i              n                 k
o                                                             f
w                           a                                r
g                  o                   o                      d
m        o    r        n       i              n               g
w                           h                                o
d                           i                                d
y                           o                                u
s                           a                                y
y                           o                                u
w                  e                   r                      e
```

148

think of the possibilities, a mathematics of words in phrases spiraling down, a
helix, the letters in the length of words, whether odd or even, is the heart of
pattern, itself, thread, hand, eye, mind, and so forth, down to the color of ones
toenail polish, weaving petro-scripts of canoes like insects from above, animals
remembered only in a species' fetal dreams, haunted caverns of patterns, broken
by sleep, etc.

```
C     r     i     s     t     o     s
r   e   t   u   r   n       t   h   y
m     e     a     s     u     r     e
s     u     n     n     e     s
s   o   u   t   h   w   a   r   d
j   o   u   r   n   e   y   s
s   p   e   n   t     s   t   i   l   l
t   h   i   s     d   o   w   n   w   a   r   d
p   u   l   s   e       m   e   n   d
t   h   y     e   a   r   t   h
a       g     a       i       n
s   t   i   t   c   h     i   t
w   i   t   h     s   w   e   e   t
f   l     o   w   e   r   s
```

or

```
C     r     i     s     t     o     s
r   e   t   u   r   n     s   h   i   n   e
f   o   r   t   h   s   t   i   l   l   t   h   y
d   o   w   n   w   a   r   d   c   o   u   r   s   e
m     o     n     t     h     s
d       e       a       d
c       o       l       d
s       t       e       m
f   r     o     z     e     n
r   e   n   e   w   t   h   y   p   r   e   s   e   n   c   e
b   r   i   n   g   w   a   r   m   t   h
s   u   n   n   e   t   o   b   e   a   r   o   n
a   l   l   t   h   y   l   i   v   i   n   g   e   a   r   t   h
```

149

paragraphs like the bending of grasses
in a soft wind,
going from one thing
to another,
the conversation of two old friends
the first night, not having
seen each other
for years

Sure Shots

–"The possibilities are finite but beyond our knowing." (Mayer) Another measure.

–Because a student recommended her, I read a book by Louise Glück. It was of no interest except as yet another example of the bad writing that is accepted, even encouraged, under the umbrella of the period style. As a child I was misdiagnosed with an ulcer and was put on a highly restrictive diet, one constant of which was milquetoast, maybe its foundation. The diet lasted for what seemed like years but was probably six months or less. At any rate, I've not been able to stand wet bread since.

–   A fish flops over,
        bright omen for New Year's Day.
        Let's do this next year.

–Plot premise for a Learning-to-Read Book for the New Millennium: *The Cat and the Mouse*. The cat is magically made out of all cheddar cheese. The mouse is made out of all mouse. The cat is very much alive, as such things are, and is hyper-sensitive to touch. A glance and pain shoots across every plain of his surface and bores into every crevice, even the teeniest, the tiniest. The mouse hypnotizes the cat into thinking he's a delicious cliff, standing statue still. The cat pleads with his eyes (If eyes could talk . . . !, etc.) [Grade 2+. All male cast. Recommended for: Coping with horror, Loss of all certainties.]

morning's run

caught out by the rain
six horses assward to wind
tails beneath their legs

This Practice Capable of Great Refinement[13]

-for Judy

vita brevis, ars longa[14]

framing the face as window the eye interlaced
with mullion, lashes or lattice, one stroke
from annihilation, brain fissure, clot, watchful
at evening that one passing (as moon) might
be known by what he bears forth, reputation
as daughter, one's issue, the loss of which
is shame, to look out straight, lustful,
frank, face in hands, despair, eye beyond
repair (what it has seen!), framing flame
in clouds' eye, reflection where head had
been, the *idea* of sight, rose as kingdoms in
such vision (and the brevity of life), castles and
capitols with broad avenues, spokes radiant from
a single source, walks into the world on two legs.

---

[13] Judy, one of my sisters, is an artist and teacher in Columbus, Ohio. During the winter of this writing, she was involved with the brush work of Chinese ideograms and radicals.

[14] An emphasis on the original sense, that of Hippocrates, as in Chaucer's "The lyf so short, the craft so long to lerne."

Barb[15]

first pussy I ever saw, the occasion was innocent almost
in way of youth, as Micah might say, as my youth was
made to compare to what I heard of hers, never the
specifics (I didn't ask nor did I care more than a typical
cousin might be concerned for a cousin at the other end
of a continent), and then the brain fissure I always forgot
but knew you were waking every morning in the same
body without remission, tied to chair and cigarettes (your
only pleasure? or did you like shitting and eating as I
do? masturbation? could you run in your mind, or was
that no remission, an intensification of your sadness?
finally two suicide attempts. all now past. after we'd
heard, my father, returning from the bathroom, asked
how he was, said sitting, "I miss Barb," looking down.

---

[15] Barbara was my cousin. Aunt Ginny had pulled the plug on
the day before she called in her bewildered grief.

Channel Surfing

The redskins nailed us ballsack to lug, a tortured
cross, lanced by steep words, a wild wind in their weapons,
rock sheer tongue of tomahawk smashing joints, cracking
heads, handles thick with gore, the day with howls and
fresh pain, overladen, only I escaped their wrath, feigning
death, losing face instead of life, I slipped away after they had
tired of their murderous sport and pulled to shore, building
fires in the evening, over which they cooked parts of my
former comrades, eating them before their very eyes, then
finally slept, and I, in great trepidation, slowly crawled
what must have been less than three-and-a-half feet
in over two hours, there being a gibbous moon, freezing
at the slightest hint of sound or stir from those red demons
who, Lord be praised, slept ever as I slipped over the side . . .

Sure Shots

–Use this as epigraph at great peril.

–What's the first word in this sentence. (An essay question.)

–About my toothache. I wouldn't mind so much if it weren't so constant, and didn't hurt.

–Tombstone for the New Millennium: It *was* all about me!

–Tombstone for the New Millennium: The world was my pussy.

–Tombstone for the New Millennium: I'm still waiting.

–Your mother and father. (I.e., a puzzle never solved.)

–from *Dating Tips for the New Millennium*: When she notices that you always seem to keep the toilet seats down at your house, say, "I'm a sensitive guy." Don't say, "I pee down the sink."

–A *Bumpersticker for the New Millennium*: Don't Botch Your Suicide

–Her face an empty mask.

Measure from here.

This sentence is the other. Softer sentence
next. One like a bucket. Then one overflowing
with eels and squid, dying and dead. On a wharf
in Scitute, Massachusetts Colony, fishing, farming,
general labor, logging, a saw mill, fruit to pick
in summer, eyes popping out all your body as you
walk into town, catching the sea full blast, deep
blue, senses reeling with morning light and the hard
rocking of all things. Master of Surfaces. More ships,
pouring England onto these shores. New pussy. Where
to find them? Friday bustle. Afternoon. By evening dead,
tangled in ropes and drowned, pulled out then dumped
upon these boards, to face your last look on light, beside
this bucket of eels and squid, dying and dead. Sunset.

Birdsong's Chant

Bear Claw told this. How Great Spirit would visit Desert many nights in the form of a huge vulture, fifty warriors high, and silently attend as Desert complained about what Sun did to her all day. Often Great Spirit would nod or grunt, as if in sympathy, but in truth he barely listened. Really, it was the same series of complaints he'd heard night after night, all these years, from nearly the beginning: Sun was a faithless bastard, He baked her brain, He smacked her barren ass, Hard, Then fucked her raw, Staked her down and pummeled her with fiery fists, Hour upon hour, Then when it got dark, he wouldn't even stay. While Desert went on and on, Great Spirit would walk and think, occasionally stopping to sigh or scratch. He would consider his many considerations, like what he should do with his latest creation, man, and whether he made the fire in him too large or too small, or what new pleasures he could invent for himself like drowning in showers of sunrise, writhing on cactus paws, quickened in silver, cold torched throughout liquid frame, mercury reflecting the sharp blood-orange glow spreading over his surface. But one night, as Desert droned on peacefully in the background, Great Spirit was preoccupied trying out his new nose. He'd worked on it for weeks, making it out of what he had laying about: a magic ball of insect parts, delicate nets fashioned out of waterfalls, ties and bindings of white bear hide, buffalo head as echo chamber, the memory of spirit bowls turning in maidens' arms, a collector, dance. Great Spirit had just attached his new nose that day with Dead Reunion Chant and sweet cactus gum. Tonight, the trial. His mind was a sacred map that held the land in place. (When he was in deepest sleep, cactus and clouds and mountains and plains and forests and lakes would shimmer, waver.) As he walked, new nose aloft, he found he could detect traces less than warm bone scent at five days' pace in the rapidly cooling air. Each "sip," rifling the slightest draught of Desert's breath, contained a strand of intricate and delicately woven fabric of such scents, winding and unwinding, woof and warp like colored lights, each strand rising from a particular place, a precise point on Great Spirit's mental map, as a wavering neon tube (some squirming), and damn!, he could see the very spot, sometimes small as a grain of sand, from which it came, the scent tube alive, wiggling free from a collapsing pore or fleck of drying plant, thick and flaccid scent from decaying flesh and bone, dried organs, fried fecal smell riding the hot copper scent of sand, all aglow deep in the sensorium woven though thousands of other such strands and rising as wave, a grand reticulum from thousands of such points in and through and with all the other strands rising from *their* delectables. Whooh!, . . . This is good shit, Great Spirit thought.

Just then the heavens shook with light and a mighty flapping as all Desert's shadows, attached only by their feet, began jerking about, this way and that, a stucco scherzo, pins staggered in long waves, wild and stuttering, Spastic Hangman's Dance, a battalion of mimes trappt in poison gas. Great Spirit, his scent trance broken, the sensual bath dissolved in the quaking air attendant upon Broken Moon's light display in descent, broad wings battering brightness from horizon to horizon, sharp scat of light over externals, his torso grown magnificent, almost unbearable. "Woah!" said Great Spirit, yet by the time he could get it out Broken Moon had already landed and perched upon his shoulder, massive as any cliff, "Could you turn that thing down?" But Broken Moon was already tucking his wings, ruffling, folding them back and in, until he was again the pleasant orb of his diurnal self, say in the lonely October sky, but now lower, with legs, talons set in Great Spirit's vast humped shoulder. As he gathered himself, light was drained of its acid baths, the interiors weaned of their intensity, and brought to a shimmering glow, which made it possible to see again without rending vision.

"Broken Moon flies down, sits on Great Spirit's shoulder," Broken Moon said, his claws tensing in the tender flesh, "It says so right there," offering for proof a brilliant wing-tip pointed to a butte, upon which Great Spirit could make out some scratchings of man, his silly nomad. Great Spirit, not wishing to appear stupid (he had not bothered to learn what such markings might mean, not having any sense that his fate could be forever bound with man's, or that such a thing could even be conceived), dully nodded. Broken Moon, however, seemed to know the script (for thus he was to call it) well. Indeed, as Great Spirit gazed into Broken Moon's obsidian eyes, wide pools of darkness wavering in light, the melody of black in lost brilliance, he could almost make out such squigglings as he saw on the rock, but *these*, at first still, static as the rock itself, gradually appeared to become animate, alive, now biomorphic forms wriggling into signs for acts of hunt, long treks, and sacrifices of dire intent changing into mute aspects of death or into weapons and the howling forms within.

Great Spirit had often thought Broken Moon responsible for this scratching habit of man. Now he was sure. *His Brilliance seemed to nose his way into my every creation*, and so it gradually dawned on him that *this* was another example of Broken Moon's attempt to permeate every crevice of *man*'s existence. Not so long ago his "quaking aberration" had been perfect, dumb and slavish, a cute pet that ate, drank, spit, shat, pissed, and copulated. He knew Broken Moon had already given man reflection, memory and meditation, thus madness, and speech for the madness, and now, he realized, he'd given him as well a way to spear and bind that speech to rock itself, forms still wiggling in tortured spasms on a fountain of flowing stone. *Unwavering madness bound in madness*, he thought. *Nothing good can come of this. This is the very worst.*

"Whoa!," Great Spirit groaned, "This is bringing me down."

But Broken Moon was already speaking, reading the squirming figures set down and out as though in memory of the future, prophetic, signs ringing sure with certain truth "'Your people will always be at war, for as many years as there are buffalo, but no tribe, ever, will be extinguished, completely gone dribbling out like a small fire or drops of piss in desert. But time will come which will make your enemies friends. No sense in this. White men, stupid of heart and tongue, appear out of a nowhere they call history'"–the figures on the rock jerked, cracked their backs and snapped their necks–"'After great victories, bitter defeat. Thus, before what's to come: Some warriors hold out, some won't and entire villages are laid waste. Bad news all around. But great tales. Acts of warriors exceeding those of the white dogs and their machines.[16] Great bravery, Bear Cat's Walk of Destruction, softly singing an ancestor chant the entire time, through the chaos of lost battle. Jumping Buffalo's slaughter of family before facing an army. A Blackfoot eating hearts of the vanquished before they cool. Death Mask leading the hard ride into his first and only skirmish at thirteen. Sacred war chant rising from Silly Crow's flames just outside fort's gate. Sore Foot, old warrior, staked

---

[26]Petroglyphic ftnt.: They will know little of spirits. Three gods living in the same house. They won't be able to watch the wind or feel the clouds rolling over and through them. They won't be able to live in dilation of sight. Their singleness of purpose will be like a blunt and stupid flood pouring over your people's lands.

out, numbering the good qualities of every pony he ever had as they whipped him to death, as he bled into the ground with hardly a sharpened intake of breath, noting the best points of each. By contrast, the white dogs collapse like dust. They're reduced to a three-year old child in less than a morning's torture. But some stories of their bravery as well, how one young colonel laughed at them for three days, told them they were worse than old, lonesome squaws as they tore him apart, piece by piece,[17] laughing (the last three hours they only heard a choked half-bark, half-croak, but they knew what it was). Now there's something to sing about!'"

"Woah!" Great Spirit was dizzy. Maybe the change of temperature. . . ? While in the background Desert droned on and on.

Broken Moon peered briefly at Great Spirit before he resumed his reading: "'Your *man* is broken at last. Rarely has a people known such defeat. Herded like Navaho sheep, sometimes weeks of walking, death from the third day, all along the trail they have to leave them with great sorrow and all hope lost, children gone so soon, survivors penned, all under the law of What Is. Meagerly kept, they will suffer great indignities. Despised, spat upon, kicked like dogs from plains to mountains to cities and back again, hard roads the whole time down which they will run, stumble, and onto which, exhausted, they will finally fall, barely stirring the 'dust' of what the white devils call History.'"

[Compare imagination to the actual, whatever it is, kingdom in every moment. How *that* actual person got in *that* doorway, for instance. What depths, sliding overlays, chambers of deep intent reside in the *actual* tales? What was their language? A tongue of coyotes and birds? Have we stripped this from them as well? And from ourselves. . . ?]

Great Spirit winced as Broken Moon's talons tightened in his shoulder. The landscape shuttered. "But worse to come," Broken Moon said looking toward the distant canyon wall, "See? They have tied their fate to yours, to

---

[17] Saving his eyes that even his god might see what we will do to him. If his torments could be witnessed by all of the white devils, every woman, child and man, they might retreat into where they came or disappear on their distant sea, that time could again begin its lonely, forgotten dance.

161

the greatness of your spirit, bound themselves to you with drawing and carving on rock like living signs for animals and warriors chipped and scraped into the stone of the world's will, signs for many-forever-gone, canoes, great buffalo, herds of beasts-all-but-forgotten, even for the words a brother whispers into his sister's ear, delicate, or for what an enemy tastes like while he's yet living, ... Until as many walls as minds in the world."

Great Spirit peered into the darkness at the distant scratching, edge of mind. As he watched, by stages curious, attentive, enwrappt, all the lines began to vibrate, each character wiggling like a stabbed insect, but more and more animate, until finally they seemed to pry themselves loose in long waves and leave the rock, rise over bluff and cliff to embed in the sky, a squirming larval neon colony, full knowing of night and decay of time, an omen-riddled dance macabre, sickness spread to rot, alive yet spiked with desiccation's very-heat-itself, singing with stinging bird fever, a seething apocalypse of signs, gruesome script beneath which even Broken Moon dimmed and Great Spirit nearly fainted. While Desert droned steadily on.

"'As your people thrive,'" Broken Moon continued after a long pause, "'you maintain your strength, the order and force of your presence, your bounds certain, your identity supreme, much meat shall be burnt for your favor, etc., but when your powers fail, as they surely will, certain as blood falls from lizard and man, downward, your influence will be as phantom water the day after a flash flood in Desert, alive in small insects, perhaps, a shit-bug or turgid weed, . . . or, perhaps, a locus someone can dip in honey, chew, eat, and swallow, to hear voices for the rest of his life'" (chants could almost be heard in the far distance), "'but that's that.'"

"This cannot be!" Great Spirit said.

"Then see for yourself!" pointing an luminous feather into night's starry depths where the script was caught in the dark, a writhing acetylene gash in Bear's Maw, and what Great Spirit saw there was seared into his brain forever. The center of each figure in the spastic script was a bobbing mouth, a dark tunnel, and the words and ideas and memories and logic and bereavements firing out and rationales for foolish pleasures and lies and staggering illuminations were brands and burning sticks that struck and stuck in all Great Spirit's mental flesh . . . until . . . he . . . passed . . .

When Great Spirit woke, and after the cacti and the buttes and the horizon gradually stabilized, he asked Broken Moon, also dazed, "Can anything be done?"

"Just one thing," Broken Moon replied, his voice weak but deepening with concern, "You must consider how to prepare a prophet when the time is right," no longer even pretending to read from the cliff. "The white devils will carry their god, Yahweh, in one package with them like sickness as they spread across your land. Now a minor demon in a distant land, this Yahweh will have grown huge, bloated on the sorrows of his people's enemies and drunk on the paucity of their own fears and hatreds. A loathsome mix. A freakin' mess. When he comes he will grab you by the crack of your neck like a small bird and hold you down, under his mighty claw, grown massive with stupid and brutal victories, spreading over many nations. He won't even listen to you. Mangy cur, heathen wad. But gradually, over several generations of men, he will loosen his hold, glance in your direction, and eventually attend. You begin to amuse him. He becomes "fond." You ask for a small salary, a few minor dispensations. For this and for your protection, you provide him, beside entertainment, one prophet for testament, . . . you could tell him it's The New Old Testament, and that his people are sliding to perdition, that he's been silent for too long, that nobody reads anymore, . . . we can think of how to embellish this, to make him afraid, how to fawn to his basest desires. . . finally tell him he could put you in charge of new communications, you'd fix it up, . . . fast. Then this Yahweh, his mind thickening with satisfactions like sweet tar deep in the inner winter of this land, will bite."

"Your words are twisting in wind. . . . I don't understand."

"But you will," Broken Moon said, and began whispering softly in Great Spirit's massive ear, "You see, . . ." [Do you remember what it was like to read when you were a child? Broken Moon's story was like that. The words had tails and the mountain was a fierce mistress, only just joking. Sentences you could sit in. Some that would warm in your lap and make strange noises. Pet you here and there. A long story. Asleep in your ear.] Stars advance in their passing. . . .

Pulling back abeam, pausing, waiting til conscious life returned to Great Spirit's eyes, . . . then a lilting moment beyond. Broken Moon said: "I'll pin him to the ground–we'll negotiate with Desert later–while you fill him full of words, . . . and wire him for sound. He'll be the mike that night might amplify your bidding into streets shining with the mistake Yahweh made when he sought to create in his own image such a mirror tortured into an 'identity,' *the solely singular,* happy, larval bloat of self amid the many, confused. . . ."

"Huh?" Great Spirit twisted and stretched his massive brow into the geography of simple befuddlement.

"Never mind. . . . I've done this before."

"How will I find him?"

"It's all arranged. I've already spoken with Circumstance and Desperation." The wall's script was now jumping around like a film shot from a camera on a run-away freight down an Appalachian mountain a madman with a handful of shit or a shuttle breaking upon re-entry when we can almost hear the screaming insides of everything, and Broken Moon was pointing and talking and waving his arms making the shadows jerk like snared animals and twisting snakes, and Desert droned on and on in the monotone of repeated complaint, tireless in tiresomeness, while Great Spirit tried to get what he could all the listening his ears might hold and mind remember like a basket some stories need to begin in the beginning which just as well could be tales now to prepare the prophet to hear what Great Spirit has to say which Broken Moon recited in great detail reflecting upon and occasionally appearing to reference the rock scratchings beyond all of which Great Spirit tried hard though in vain to remember not being simply illiterate but also because the script kept moving squirming and jerking in paroxysms of hieroglyph's hysterical riddle-nature while he looked at it harder and strained to grasp and keep what moved so swiftly with erratic words like insane bats stories that snuff themselves in dead alleys and gully whoppers with muffled screams and bloodied feathers though it seemed Broken Moon spoke some things more often than not and gradually enough Great Spirit could feel these "things" more like distempered rodents mucking and monkeying about inside his cranium and feel them going through the portal of his ears down the myriad conduits into his inner chambers resonating with the grim drift: empty this your body like stale beer pour out your hopes and fears the worse is before you no man will know more despair yet in your darkest hours amid strangers–an ignorant callous hostile and malicious people–know that I shall send one who will come before you and be with and follow after almost as I am hard upon you like a cliff a hard edge beyond which there are no concessions nor satisfactions when I pick you up to speak you better be ready I don't apologize for nothing you will be ridiculed by the intelligent feared by the stupid shunned by the most despised and *all* other prophets with their idols and you saddled like a stupid bitch with a half-breed god yet be hard as flint for there is darker yet to come you will have to learn the core of flames' most intimate mind heart of the meaning of fire prime self-wringing anguish but know in thy throes that song shall save thee extinguish pain be comforted there is great call and bewilderment before you above all be ready to listen when Broken Moon holds you down by the shoulders and drills you while I drool these words softly in your ear the one you hear with then what shall I say but what I will know as my body and with all my being. At this Broken Moon again leaned into Great Sprit's cavernous ear as the script burnt a flaming cartouche, squirming fibers of light, organisms flying through scorching air and into the visual cortex of night with its fiery brand beneath a vault yet echoing with the monstrous screams of the beginning.

A wreathe of smoke rose silently mid-prairie which could be seen half-a-days' distance, as Desert droned steadily on.

No song more.

Sure Shots

–"I envy you your first reading of this book." Another Blurb for the New Millennium. (Conceived while reading Stanford's *The Battlefield Where the Moon Says I Love You*, but applicable to many other books as well.[10])

–Plotinus sat down, his feet in the pool, and wept. The wonder was there was anything left. The orb had cooled, settled into the steady rocking of his thought. Nothing begins where word ends. Nothing to stanch his weeping.

–Blurb for the New Millennium: Like making love with a guppy.

–Maledictum for the New Millennium: I'd write an elegy for you if I thought it'd do any good.

–"The Galibis of Guiana, when asked the meaning of their curious funeral ceremony, which consists of dancing on the grave, they replied they did it to stamp down the earth." (Encyclopedia Britannica, 11th ed., vol 7, p. 899). The Brits were always gullible, and they basically hated themselves.

---

[10] I'll not bugger it with titles.

and the capitol is lost, avenues crumble
beneath the weight of our leaving, potholes
laugh in our wake. pine needles will glow in the
dark, keeping small rodents asleep throughout
the night until the owls and the hawks and the
snakes all starve. but we've lost them long since
anyway. where once stood such presences (on
tongue, in minds), now cavort as cartoons, the fifth
importations of lame conceptions, lassitude
of thought. pry open a casket and prepare to be
blasted by a laughter so rancid it will scorch your
face, and "catch your hair on fire." and the police
will finally do what they've always wanted to do.
with guns. maybe. maybe not. maybe it's stuck
together below our knowing, before making
ourselves known, maybe before the morning
Adam was stuck naming, coelacanth, *Struthio*
camelus, *Pyrus malus*, the fruit of which takes
nourishment at source, forbidden, site from which
totems rise. Green as a green sea on a green day
asleep while waking. I mean it has a gleam,
shard of flint in its eye like the sheen of tired
failure surrounding a middle-aged actor as a mis-
shapen nimbus or caul in yet another monster-rises-
from-the-depths movie, they handed you green
glasses as they herded you past, and 15 minutes
in everything reverses, shadows disappear into their referents (which can only be known
by *their* shadows, etc., stupid movie buzzing in
your cortex a ditty about a place where reversals
are themselves reversed, irrevocably, final and
continuous, changing everything otherwise all the
same or a difference in kind, and at once, nearly
never or always as time?, you can't remember,
but now the ship's bobbing throws you helplessly
about the sides of the room rocking the head you are

in, what bubbles are for, fastidiously is so furious
and delicate as death (and as subtle), that is you're
smashed, and the otherwise flaccid lines lash your
face with the singular intensity of iced spittle in
storm-driven winds, as the vast mug of monster rises
in its green silvery flesh, factitiously actualized. *that*
green. and utterly fertile, ripe zero, that is, almost
never not quite nearly enough, *the possibilities are*
finite, yet beyond our knowing, as just after the last
neuronal flicker in brainstem, core, night's pregnant
city under fire from afar, stars on the rim, its silence
amplified, the peripheries "stuffed," alive, and
beneath it all a swirling confluence of what is
with what is not, the infinite saturating "instance,"
liquid as light, permeating each particulate,
chasms of anchors in such seas, and a leviathan
conceived in mute austerity, facing down, as
it were, the elements of experience, *their* sheen,
unremitting, the stupidity of what happens all
the time, yet borne on the backs of dolphins, from
the antithetical center, whose circle is everywhere,
the self a verdancy of such connections, purpose
wired to its ancient completion. unbinding otherwise.

for what in their passing

mind in hand words hold, or
tenders them touch as they pulse
toward invisible arm from shadow
of shoulder, the mind a city of such
shadows, words floating down
alleys, up avenues, curling thru
open slips of door, riding slices of
wind to hurl themselves, crazed,
at the ear, adrift in restaurants, bars,
in stations, hallways, rooms and
cubicles, flung from cars, spat out
into the street by the destitute, into
the cold street, the hot street, you must
be dispossessed, they say, to know
anything, what the curb feels of a cheek,
so hungry you forget to chew properly
or your jaw breaks from constant
clinching, words like ripe loogies,
bait to spit on passing legs, *wish*
you had enough for every bastard,
words fracturing arms, burnt
socket, sharp notions of noggins
splintering, and for the amputation
of hands which had only just held them
in their passing for such moment, as
one, longing to begin, touches another,
also longing, now orphaned, they do
what they want, and have to, sucking
cock, stealing ain't nothing, lying don't
even register, they let old men drill them
in the ass for the price of a meal, a cup
of coffee, a vacation from the pavement, sit
quiet while glowing in their exposure a few
minutes from the hard streets amid
words of thieves and liars, words for
hire, pimping their own mothers, bright

squalor of thought festering like words
in all the furthest crevasses of every
city, hands bereft of words, arms, shadows
of shoulders looming above like
the inversion of clouds, bright mist
blooming beneath, beyond which the mind
that might have recognized them as the lovely
creatures they are or might be if alive, informed
by experience, instructed of the mist, held softly
by shadow, arm, and hand, breathing soft
breezes of the possible, location of solace,
meditative cohesion of the self, etc., a word
accurately tho provisionally applied, instead
of this instrument for gain, manipulation,
delivery and support of the misbegotten
conception you see before you in the glass
as you tie off the cord, the umbilicus
sliding through you hand, and in your mind . . .

. . . difference in kind, and *naturally,* or

nearly almost nominally so? "You can only get there from here," he said, "if you realize where you are, living. Here *is* there in its vast unfolding though death's at the root of everything," he continued, "the skull a *pomme de terre* milked dry by life's tentacles, otherwise simply the current receptacle for swarms of lies, hatreds, fears, confusions of spirit fattened on harvests of bitter disappointment, or fat & flaccid with dithering lunacies beneath a face stamped on an enervating grin. A story of stones & fists," he laughed, "where risks are actual, falls final, & pain sweet as-the-balls-of-Baby-Jesus real." Then casting me an eye, "Yet here," he touched my chest, "graces come for nourishment, & mind drinks deep & all kinds are redefined. Is never shut from you, never dead until it's dead."

These are peaks

shimmer in the distance, midwinter's sun on
snow, acidic light bathing in retinas' pools, slowly
they revolve, dissolve in wide summer's air, then
disappear. Gone as a dead man's dream. Song. All
night peaks in the brain, afternoons ashudder. Bowl
of emptiness in cupboard. "And why not," cried the ram,
"kill the boy in *my* stead? Nothing but trouble can come
of him." (Pound told me this joke. He called it Wisdom
of Beasts. Deep crevasse, brains shattered on what abyss,
and yet the Alps, as Bunting wrote, you can always
try to go around. These peaks revolve beneath our
feet, shelter in the darkness of our dreams, demand
as seasons, our allegiance, to follow what orders into
what skies? There's always a choice.

Word at morning

bronze grackles   &   blackbirds
in their unsettling   before dawn   in the bamboo grove
to which

     I have come   (in mine)   to sound

     in their sound   dark cacophonies   conjunction of
creature-in-

     creature need   wide mewing, clucking, crying   and
clicking   that rattle   in the predawn   echo
     of

     their splashing

     off opposing tangle of
     life / lives
     then a brief diminution   as clusters rise
into the upper reaches of two pear trees which have been swallowed
the bamboo   lost in their attentions
     then as loud as previous

     such pulsing   two or
     three times   before
     a deep, sudden hush
     (like a dead man catching his breath)
     and the first string   peels out
     west

     goddamned beautiful fucking
     tube, wavering,   stretching   for
     miles   anywhere from four
     to over twenty individuals   deep   as they exit
sometimes in clouds   thicker tubes   pulsing

     then I saw
     a hawk   not fifteen yards distant   at
     my height   patrolling the coulee
     surely   with so much life   there must be
     glorious accidents

     light in all the branches

he flies back and forth every few minutes
            finally the tube is pinched off   inexplicably
    surely   like a good shit
        I hear thousands more   yet in the grove
                    their music rises
            splashes over light, pink on verge of orange
                                    mere yellow
            leaking into the east

                        Dawn Patrol
                                    flies back
                            and forth
                        once more

    then they hush again   and a thick   pulsing   cloud comes out
            pulling another tube   even thicker than the first
                    more miles of birds   scat into distance
        and while I'm reading their wavering script   it runs backward
            like spokes of film   as language in dream
                        then
            a tube to the north   also headed west   from the grove
        behind the carport   now flows into the first   and I
            am surrounded in birds'   near circle woven
                    script   in   motion   glowing
            just like on television   trying to read
                        blest?   or cursed?

    .

                    as hawk sits his tree
                                    watching

to remain throughout

oblivion spun of absence into a fine liquid strand, deepest purple, almost black, poured into an opening at the top of your skull, you of course are transparent, shivering as the thread plunges into your cranium, also of liquid, translucent, a dream's definition of *stealth*, widens as it slows, then the slightest feathers of purple slide from the strand, unfurl to permeate your every crevice, impossible that the body should bear, the weight of it!, absence grounded in the actual, brute stare, even your saliva stinks of it, a little hand caresses your nutsack as you feel *an exploratory finger*, that is, you'll go on missing them forever, a gray word like cement into the soft velvet glove of predawn as westward grackles fly, also into such weather, dark calculus of being, what's not going away

OTHER TITLES FROM AHADADA

Ahadada Books publishes poetry. Preserving the best of the small press tradition, we produce finely designed and crafted books in limited editions.

Bela Fawr's Cabaret (David Annwn)   978-0-9808873-2-7

Writes Gavin Selerie: "David Annwn's work drills deep into strata of myth and history,. exposing devices which resonate in new contexts. Faithful to the living moment, his poems dip, hover and dart through soundscapes rich with suggestion, rhythmically charged and etymologically playful. Formally adventurous and inviting disjunction, these texts retain a lyric coherence that powerfully renders layers of experience. The mode veers from jazzy to mystical, evoking in the reader both disturbance and content. *Bela Fawr's Cabaret* has this recognisable stamp: music and legend 'Knocked Abaht a Bit', mischievous humour yielding subtle insight."

Age of the Demon Tools (Mark Spitzer)   978-0-9808873-1-0

Writes Ed Sanders: "You have to slow down, and absorb calmly, the procession of gritty, pointillist gnarls of poesy that Mark Spitzer wittily weaves into his book. Just the title, *Age of the Demon Tools*, is so appropriate in this horrid age of inappropriate technology—you know, corruptly programmed voting machines, drones with missiles hovering above huts, and mind reading machines looming just a few years into the demon-tool future. When you do slow down, and tarry within Spitzer's neologism-packed litanies, you will find the footprints of bards such as Allen Ginsberg, whose tradition of embedding current events into the flow of poesy is one of the great beacons of the new century. This book is worth reading if only for the poem 'Unholy Millenial Litany' and its blastsome truths."

Sweet Potatoes (Lou Rowan)   978-0-9781414-5-5

Lou Rowan . . . is retired, in love and charged. He was raised by horse breeders and went to Harvard and thus possesses an outward polish. But he talks like a radical, his speech incongruous with his buttoned-down appearance. *Golden Handcuffs Review*, the local literary magazine that Rowan founded and edits, is much like the man himself: appealing and presentable on the outside, a bit wild and experimental at the core.

Deciduous Poems (David B. Axelrod)   978-0-9808873-0-3

Dr. David B. Axelrod has published hundreds of articles and poems as well as sixteen books of poetry. Among his many grants and awards, he is recipient of three Fulbright Awards including his being the first official Fulbright Poet-in-Residence in the People's Republic of China. He was featured in Newsday as a "Star in his academic galaxy," and characterized by the New York Times as "a treat." He has shared the stage with such notables as Louis Simpson, X. J. Kennedy, William Stafford, Robert Bly, Allen Ginsburg, David Ignatow and Galway Kinnell, in performance for the U.N., the American Library Association, the Struga Festival, and hundreds more schools and public events. His poetry has been translated into fourteen languages and he is a frequent and celebrated master teacher.

Late Poems of Lu You (Burton Watson)   978-0-9781414-9-3

Lu You (1125–1210) whose pen name was 'The Old Man Who Does as He Pleases,' was among the most prolific of Chinese poets, having left behind a collection of close to ten thousand poems as well as miscellaneous prose writings. His poetry, often characterized by an intense patriotism, is also notable for its recurrent expression of a carefree enjoyment of life. This volume consists of twenty-five of Burton Watson's new translations, plus Lu You's poems as they appear in the original, making this a perfect collection for the lay reader as well as for those with a mastery of Song dynasty Chinese.

www.ahadada.com

Oulipoems (Philip Terry)   978-0-978-1414-2-4

Philip Terry was born in Belfast in 1962 and has been working with Oulipian and related writing practices for over twenty years. His lipogrammatic novel *The Book of Bachelors* (1999), was highly praised by the Oulipo: "Enormous rigour, great virtuosity—but that's the least of it." Currently he is Director of Creative Writing at the University of Essex, where he teaches a graduate course on the poetics of constraint. His work has been published in *Panurge*, *PN Review*, *Oasis*, *North American Review* and *Onedit*, and his books include the celebrated anthology of short stories *Ovid Metamorphosed* (2000) and *Fables of Aesop* (2006). His translation of Raymond Queneau's last book of poems, *Elementary Morality*, is forthcoming from Carcanet. *Oulipoems* is his first book of poetry.

The Impossibility of Dreams (David Axelrod)   978-0-9781414-3-1

Writes Louis Simpson: "Whether Axelrod is reliving a moment of pleasure, or a time of bitterness and pain, the truth of his poetry is like life itself compelling." Dr. David B. Axelrod has published hundreds of articles and poems as well as sixteen books of poetry. Among his many grants and awards, he is recipient of three Fulbright Awards including his being the first official Fulbright Poet-in-Residence in the People's Republic of China . He was featured in *Newsday* as a "Star in his academic galaxy," and characterized by the *New York Times* as "A Treat." His poetry has been translated into fourteen languages and he is a frequent and celebrated master teacher.

Now Showing (Jim Daniels)   0-9781414-1-5

Of Jim Daniels, the *Harvard Review* writes, "Although Daniels' verse is thematically dark, the energy and beauty of his language and his often brilliant use of irony affirm that a lighter side exists. This poet has already found his voice. And he speaks with that rare urgency that demands we listen." This is affirmed by Carol Muske, who identifies the "melancholy sweetness" running through these poems that identifies him as "a poet born to praise".

China Notes & The Treasures of Dunhuang (Jerome Rothenberg)   0-9732233-9-1

"*The China Notes* come from a trip in 2002 that brought us out as far as the Gobi Desert & allowed me to see some of the changes & continuities throughout the country. I was traveling with poet & scholar Wai-lim Yip & had a chance to read poetry in five or six cities & to observe things as part of an ongoing discourse with Wai-lim & others. The ancient beauty of some of what we saw played out against the theme park quality of other simulacra of the past....A sense of beckoning wilderness/wildness in a landscape already cut into to serve the human need for power & control." So Jerome Rothenberg describes the events behind the poems in this small volume—a continuation of his lifelong exploration of poetry and the search for a language to invoke the newness and strangeness both of what we observe and what we can imagine.

The Passion of Phineas Gage & Selected Poems (Jesse Glass)   0-9732233-8-3

The Passion of Phineas Gage & Selected Poems presents the best of Glass' experimental writing in a single volume. Glass' ground-breaking work has been hailed by poets as diverse as Jerome Rothenberg, William Bronk and Jim Daniels for its insight into human nature and its exploration of forms. Glass uses the tools of postmodernism: collaging, fragmentation, and Oulipo-like processes along with a keen understanding of poetic forms and traditions that stretches back to Beowulf and beyond. Moreover, Glass finds his subject matter in larger-than-life figures like Phineas Gage—the man whose life was changed in an instant when an iron bar was sent rocketing through his brain in a freak accident—as well as in ants processing up a wall in time to harpsichord music in order to steal salt crystals from the inner lip of a cowrie shell. The range and ambition of his work sets it apart. The product of over 30 years of engagement with the avant-garde, *The Passion of Phineas Gage & Selected Poems* is the work of a mature poet who continues to reinvent himself with every text he produces.

www.ahadada.com

*aha***dada**

b o o k s

tokyo / toronto

Send a request to be added to our mailing list:
http://www.ahadadabooks.com/

Ahadada Books are available from these fine distributors:

Canada
Ahadada Books
3158 Bentworth Drive
Burlington, Ontario
Canada, L7M 1M2
Phone: (905) 617-7754
http://www.ahadadabooks.com

United States of America
Small Press Distribution
1341 Seventh Street
Berkeley, CA 94710-1409
Phone: (510) 524-1668
Fax: (510) 524-0852
http://www.spdbooks.org/

Europe
West House Books
40 Crescent Road
Nether Edge, Sheffield
United Kingdom S7 1HN
Phone: 0114-2586035
http://www.westhousebooks.co.uk/

Japan
Intercontinental Marketing Corp.
Centre Building 2nd floor
1-14-13 Iriya, Taitoku
Tokyo 110-0013
Telephone 81-3-3876-3073
http://www.imcbook.net/